PHL

KU-724-235

54060000220839

STARTING RIGHT

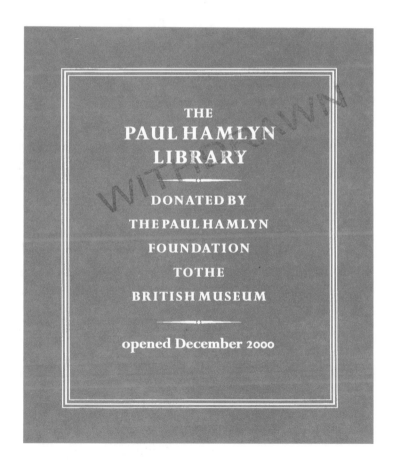

THE
PAUL HAMLYN
LIBRARY

DONATED BY
THE PAUL HAMLYN
FOUNDATION
TO THE
BRITISH MUSEUM

opened December 2000

AMERICAN ASSOCIATION FOR STATE AND LOCAL HISTORY BOOK SERIES

SERIES EDITOR
Beth Luey
Arizona State University

EDITORIAL ADVISORY BOARD
J.D. Britton, Ohio Historical Society
David Donath, Woodstock Foundation, Inc.
D. Stephen Elliott, Council for America's First Freedom
Max J. Evans, National Historical Publications and Records Commission
Cynthia Koch, Franklin D. Roosevelt Library-Museum
Tom Mason, Indiana Historical Society
Karla Nicholson, Kentucky Historical Society
Lynne Poirier-Wilson, Asheville Art Museum & Independent Consultant
John Schleicher, McGoogan Library of Medicine
Marjorie Schwarzer, Museum Studies, John F. Kennedy University
James Vaughan, National Trust for Historic Preservation

ABOUT THE SERIES
The American Association for State and Local History Book Series publishes technical and professional information for those who practice and support history, and addresses issues critical to the field of state and local history. To submit a proposal or manuscript to the series, please request proposal guidelines from AASLH headquarters: AASLH Book Series, 1717 Church St., Nashville, Tennessee 37203. Telephone: (615) 320-3203. Fax: (615) 327-9013. Web site: www.aaslh.org.

ABOUT THE ORGANIZATION
The American Association for State and Local History (AASLH) is a nonprofit educational organization dedicated to advancing knowledge, understanding, and appreciation of local history in the United States and Canada. In addition to sponsorship of this book series, the Association publishes the periodical *History News*, a newsletter, technical leaflets and reports, and other materials; confers prizes and awards in recognition of outstanding achievement in the field; and supports a broad education program and other activities designed to help members work more effectively. To join the organization, contact: Membership Director, AASLH, 1717 Church St., Nashville, Tennessee 37203.

STARTING RIGHT

A Basic Guide to Museum Planning

GERALD GEORGE
AND
CINDY SHERRELL-LEO

SECOND EDITION BY
GERALD GEORGE

ALTAMIRA
PRESS

A Division of Rowman & Littlefield Publishers, Inc.
Walnut Creek • Lanham • New York • Toronto • Oxford

THE BRITISH MUSEUM

THE PAUL HAMLYN LIBRARY

069.0973 GEO

WITHDRAWN

ALTAMIRA PRESS
A division of the Rowman & Littlefield Publishers, Inc.
1630 North Main Street, #367, Walnut Creek, CA 94596
www.altamirapress.com

Rowman & Littlefield Publishers, Inc.
A whollly owned subsidiary of The Roman & Littlefield Publishing Group, Inc.
4501 Forbes Boulevard, Suite 200, Lanham, MD 20706

PO Box 317, Oxford, OX2 9RU, UK

The editorial preparation of this book was made possible by funds from the Bay Foundation.

Copyright © 2004 by ALTAMIRA PRESS

All rights reserved. No part of this publication may be reproduced, stored in a retrieval system, or transmitted in any form or by any means, electronic, mechanical, photocopying, recording, or otherwise, without the prior permission of the publisher.

British Library Cataloguing in Publication Information Available

Library of Congress Cataloging-in-Publication Data

George, Gerald, (Gerald W.)
   Starting right : a basic guide to museum planning Gerald George and Cindy Sherrell-Leo. — 2nd ed.
      p. cm. — (American Association for State and Local History book series)
   Includes index.
   ISBN 0-7591-0556-1 (hardcover : alk. paper)—ISBN 0-7591-0557-X (pbk. : alk. paper)
   1. Museums—United States—Handbooks, manuals, etc. I. Title. II. Series.

   AM11.G46 2004
   069'.0973—dc22

                        2003022146

Printed in the United States of America

♾™ The paper used in this publication meets the minimum requirements of American National Standard for Information Sciences—Permanence of Paper for Printed Library Materials, ANSI/NISO Z39.48-1992.

Contents

PART III

Some Basic Documents

A

Basic Organization Chart, 129

B

Board Membership Responsibilities Agreement, 131

C

Sample Museum Bylaws, 133

D

Typical Museum Budget List, 141

E

Sample Position Description for a Director, 143

F

Sample Certificate of Gift, 145

G

Standard Object Cataloging Record, 147

Index, 149

About the Authors, 157

Preface: Getting a Museum Going

Does one of the following describe who you are and what has brought you to this book?

You are a conscientious citizen who got mad when somebody threatened to tear down the handsome old passenger-train depot that has been a landmark in your town for decades. You led a successful fight to save it. You proposed to make it into a museum of history, science, or art.

Or, your community or group is about to celebrate a significant anniversary such as a centennial. You have agreed to head a committee to decide how to observe the occasion. Your committee recommended creating a museum to preserve some part of the historic, artistic, or natural heritage of your group or community.

Or, you are the president of a local or regional historical society. Someone has just given it a wonderful collection of wearing apparel from earlier times, a huge file of historical photographs, or an attic full of antique furniture. There is just no room to display any of this in your historical society's office, library, or meeting room. You decide that the time has come for the society to expand by developing a museum.

Or, you chair the tourism development committee of your community's chamber of commerce. On a recent visit to another community you found yourself fascinated by its museum. You believe that your city could attract more tourists if it, too, had a museum. You have persuaded the chamber to take the lead to get one started.

Or, you are connected with a local or regional parks department. It has just been given a historic site with one or more buildings on it. You are involved in preserving and interpreting the site. You need to explain the site's natural or historical significance to visitors. You plan to use one of the buildings for a visitor center with museum exhibits.

Or, you are, or know, an archaeologist who has just finished an interesting dig, which turned up a lot of prehistoric artifacts or battleground relics. You want to develop a permanent public repository for their study and display.

Or, you recognize that there is an underrepresented community in your area with a history that has been ignored. You want to collect artifacts for a museum that will explain that community's history and culture to its own members and to the larger society.

Or, you work in an archival institution, a library, a college, or a university whose possessions include a collection of, say, art objects, old letters, early-day medical equipment, or preserved natural specimens. You would like to create a museum to display the collection.

Or, you are a private collector who would like to give the fine collection you have assembled over the years to your community—if you could be sure that the community would keep your collection safe in perpetuity. You want to help the community create a museum that can preserve your collection and exhibit it.

Are any of these descriptions close?

If so, this book is for you. It can be useful to anyone who needs a nontechnical introduction to museums and their operations. We have been told that some museums give copies of this book to new board members, that some museum professionals use it in training docents and other volunteers, and that some professors include it in readings for museum studies and public history courses. This book's purpose is to help anyone who lacks a museum background but is taking on museum responsibilities, particularly anyone who is considering creating a new museum.

If you are such a person, your situation is similar to that of many others in our society. Americans have been founding museums at an astounding rate. In 1910, the United States had some 600 museums; by the mid-1980s, the number had exceeded 6,000. By the end of the 1980s, a study made for the National Trust for Historic Preservation indicated the existence of that many historic house museums alone. By 2003, the *Official Museum Directory*, published by the American Association of Museums, contained more than 8,000 listings. And the 2001 edition of the *Directory of Historical Organizations in the United States and Canada*, compiled by the American Association for State and Local History, had more than 10,000 entries, many of them museums or historical organizations that include history museums. The number of museums in operation today considerably exceeds 10,000 if one includes all the kinds defined by the Institute of Museum and Library Services (IMLS): a federal government agency, as eligible for its grants, "[A]quariums, arboreta and botanical gardens, art museums, youth museums, general museums, historic houses and sites, history museums, nature centers, natural history and anthropology museums, planetariums, science and technology centers, specialized museums and zoological parks." Americans, it seems, have been seized with museum mania. One goal of this book is to keep that pleasant state from deteriorating into museum mayhem through the creation of museums that are poorly operated or cannot be sustained.

So many wonderful museums are now open to the public. In the United States, just to give a few examples, they range from the Guggenheim in New York to the Getty in Los Angeles among major art museums; from Baltimore's National Aquarium to the San Diego Zoo among museums of live specimens; from Colonial Williamsburg's restoration of an entire eighteenth-century Virginia town to Old World Wisconsin's collection of pioneer buildings; from Historic Fort Snelling in Minnesota to the USS *Arizona* Memorial in Pearl Harbor; from Rochester's Strong Museum, the "national museum of play," with its National Toy Hall of Fame to the Children's Discovery Museum in San Jose, California; and from the Alexander & Baldwin Sugar Museum in Hawaii to the Sloss Furnaces National Historic Landmark in Birmingham. Historic building museums range from George Washington's Mount Vernon in Virginia and Paul Revere's house in Boston to the Lower East Side Tenement Museum in New York City and the 1950s' All-Electric House at the Johnson County Museum of History (Kansas). Also, there is the Colby College Museum of Art in Waterville, Maine, Living History Farms near Des Moines, Iowa; Shaker Village of Pleasant Hill, Kentucky; the Jewish Museum of Florida in Miami Beach; the African American Museum in Philadelphia; the Alutiiq Museum and Archaeological Repository in Kodiak, Alaska; Chicago's Field Museum of natural history; and the Civil War battlefield museums of the National Park Service. Most states now maintain large, multifaceted museums. Also, regional museums have developed such as the Panhandle-Plains Historical Museum in Canyon, Texas, and the Historical Museum of Southern Florida in Miami. And hundreds of city, town, and county museums have taken their places beside colleges, schools, and libraries as cultural resources for their communities.

Unfortunately, many museums also are struggling. You have only to look around your region to find one or more looking down-at-the-heels, uncompetitive with other attractions, uninspiring to the few visitors who come, and approaching insolvency. In 2002, this condition had become so chronic, particularly among historic houses, that Richard Moe, president of the National Trust for Historic Preservation, publicly asked the preservation field to consider whether there might be too many house museums. In the same year, the National Trust for Historic Preservation and the American Association for State and Local History jointly sponsored a conference entitled "Rethinking the Historic House Museum for the 21st Century." Many museums begin with historic structures, so that conference's "rethinking" is reflected in this book. By "starting right," you have a better chance of avoiding the regrettable malaise that afflicts too many museums.

Sustainable, meaningful museums are wonderful community assets and give joy to their creators as well as to their visitors. In a short reading time, this book explains what someone who is not a trained museum professional needs to know before starting a museum or expanding one. What is required to make a museum successful? What are the steps to take in order to achieve success? What are the kinds of costs, the legal responsibilities, the potential problems, and the hidden pitfalls? The hope is to prepare you by identifying all major concerns that your planning needs to take into consideration.

Part of that preparation is to let you know where to find additional sources of how-to-do-it information that are more detailed. Many good books, technical leaflets, and websites are available on various aspects of museum work, along with other kinds of practical assistance. Numerous state, regional, and national organizations provide help. At the end of each chapter, you will find selective lists of other publications and resources pertinent to topics covered in the chapter. (Although some out-of-print publications are still useful, nearly every resource cited here was available from a publisher at the time of this revision's preparation.)

In describing museum work, this book will introduce you to some unfamiliar terms that have special meanings to museum professionals. No glossary is included because the text itself tries to provide understandable explanations. But if here or in your other reading about museums you encounter an insufficiently explained term, you will likely find it defined in a museum glossary provided by the Registrars Committee of the American Association of Museums (www.rcaam.org).

A large proportion of museums in the United States are history museums, to one degree or another, and many began as community projects, focusing on the heritage of the group to which the museum founders belonged or the place where they lived. Therefore, the advice and illustrations in this book are particularly pertinent to community history museums. This short work will not adequately introduce you to the needs of some of the kinds of museums identified in the previously mentioned IMLS grant-eligibility list, such as zoos, aquariums, botanical gardens, and children's museums. But the principles identified here are pertinent to museums of many kinds.

Overall, this book is designed to help you evaluate your prospects and, if they are sufficient, to help you create a sound, practical museum-development plan. No book can make someone a museum expert, but basic guidance at the outset, including where to find expertise, can keep your dream of a fine museum from turning into a frustrating nightmare. People like you who have taken time to look into museum requirements in advance and planned well to meet them have ultimately won applause from their communities and have found museum development among the most meaningful, satisfying experiences of their lives.

May that happy result be yours!

For More Information

Your own state's museum association or historical society or agency, which is likely to be located in your state's capital city, may have lists of museums that are relatively close to you and information about exemplary ones. For a national look at established museums of many kinds and sizes, consult the most recent *Official Museum Directory*, published by the American Association of Museums, and the most recent versions of the *Directory of Historical Organizations in the United States and Canada* and the *Directory of Historic House Museums in the United States*, published by AltaMira Press.

Also, you can identify particularly accomplished museums near you or of interest for your purposes by consulting the following sources of information:

- For winners of the National Award for Museum Service, contact the Institute of Museum and Library Services, Office of Museum Services, 1100 Pennsylvania Ave., NW, Room 609, Washington, DC 20506, (202) 606-8536, www .imls.gov

- For award-winning history museums, contact the American Association for State and Local History, 1717 Church Street, Nashville, TN 37203, (615) 320-3203, www .aaslh.org

- For accredited museums, consult the American Association of Museums, 1575 Eye St., NW, Suite 400, Washington, DC 20005, (202) 289-1818, www.aam-us.org

- For respected historic house museums, varied examples are maintained in networks by such professional organizations as the National Trust for Historic Preservation, 1785 Massachusetts Ave., NW, Washington, DC 20036, (202) 588-6000, www.nthp.org; and the Society for the Preservation of New England Antiquities, 141 Cambridge St., Boston, MA 02114, (617) 227-3956, www.spnea.org

Acknowledgments

The first edition of this book appeared in 1986 in consequence of a lot of phone calls from people who needed advice on starting museums. The calls came to the office of the American Association for State and Local History, of which I was then director, and they came to the offices of state and regional historical organizations, museum associations, and preservation organizations, including the Texas Historical Commission, where Cindy Sherrell-Leo directed the Museum and Field Services Department. Recognizing the need for a book of basics that we could put in the hands of community museum developers, Cindy joined me as coauthor of the first edition and has graciously and helpfully contributed to this revision. I greatly thank her, her husband, Jack Leo, who contributed material added to this edition on museum security, and our mutual friend, Sam Hoyle, who provided information on military museums.

Though I, alone, am responsible for any shortcomings in this version, this revision is better because of helpful criticism from Max van Balgooy and several anonymous reviewers recruited by AltaMira Press. I thank Mary van Balgooy for permission to use the Board Membership Responsibilities form that she developed. I am grateful to Susan Walters, manuscript acquisitions and development at AltaMira, for help of numerous kinds. Additionally, I owe gratitude to Terry Davis, president and CEO of the American Association for State and Local History, for securing and administering the grant that supported this revision; to James Vaughan, vice president for stewardship of historic properties of the National Trust for Historic Preservation, who encouraged and supported the grant application; to Deanna Marcum, who, while president of the Council on Library and Information Resources, allowed me leave from my work there to do this revision; and doubly to Robert Ashton, executive director of the Bay Foundation, who provided grant support for the first edition and another grant that made this revision possible.

Also, for help and encouragement, I thank my favorite museum (and archives) professional, my wife, Carol Maryan-George, to whom, with love, I dedicate this edition.

GERALD GEORGE

PART I

WHAT YOU NEED TO KNOW ABOUT IT

The 1950s All-Electric House. The Johnson County (Kansas) Museums organization, which interprets suburban growth among other aspects of history, preserves this house. Photo courtesy of Johnson County Museums and Dan Fruesh Photography.

1

Respect Is the Overall Rule

What makes a good museum?

There are good museums of many kinds in many places. But they have one thing in common. They put us in contact with real things—"tangible objects," in the words of the national Museum and Library Services Act—a Vincent van Gogh painting, a fabulous jewel, a living tortoise, a stuffed elephant, a tyrannosaurus rex's skeleton, a Civil War sword, a bee hive, a Victorian house, a spinning wheel in operation, the eye of a fly seen under magnification, a functioning engine rigged up for demonstration, the desk where Abraham Lincoln signed the Emancipation Proclamation, and that historic document itself. Except perhaps for museums that keep objects only so long as they are used in teaching, there is one underlying principle of museum organization and operation: *respect for the "real thing."* One could define a museum as an organization for evaluating and explaining the value of real things. A good museum is one in which respect for the real things that it has taken into its care underlies everything it does.

What exactly does this mean?

A simple example will illustrate. Imagine that you are on a visit to see a rather common and uncomplicated kind of museum exhibit. To break down the old notion that a museum is necessarily a building, envision this imaginary exhibit as housed in a "history van" that has just arrived in your community, on tour from your state museum or historical society. Assume also that the van is taking exhibits around to commemorate an anniversary such as your state's beginning as a U.S. territory.

As you enter, one of the first things you see in the exhibit is an ancient clay pot, beautiful in shape and fascinatingly decorated. Such an artifact makes a good illustration because prehistoric pottery is commonly found in museums of many kinds: museums of art, science, history, and archaeology; ethnic museums; community museums; and even museums for children. (Indeed, an entrancing pot—a "stirrup jug"—ingeniously encircled by the lifelike tentacles of an octopus painted on it in Crete fifteen hundred years before Christ is on display near a living octopus in the National Zoo in Washington, D.C.!)

Suppose that our imaginary clay pot came from an archaeological dig in your state and was made by some of its earliest inhabitants. On your visit, you learn such things by reading a sign (or *label*, as museum people would call it) on the glass-enclosed case in which the pot is protected and displayed. Or you hear about the pot's significance from a guide (or *docent*, as museum people say), who takes groups through the exhibit. Or you learn about it from listening to the tape in the audio guide that you rented or borrowed when you came in. Or you get explanatory information from an interactive video accompanying the exhibit.

From one or more of these sources, you learn about the culture of the people who made the pot, how they made it, where they lived, how they used it, what its decorations may have signified, what became of its creators, and what archaeologists do and do not understand about them. Your feeling for this piece of shaped clay begins to expand beyond curiosity as you realize just how old it is and what a window it constitutes into another world, which you try to imagine with the help of a photograph behind it of the dwelling ruins in which it was found and an artist's sketch of how those dwellings and their people might once have looked.

Now think about all this from a museum viewpoint. Somebody clearly has gone to great trouble to make the viewing of that piece of pottery a significant experience for you. Someone wanted to share with you an appreciation of a valued object—its rarity, beauty, originality, and craftsmanship. Someone wanted to invoke the potential of that object to fill gaps in understanding a part of human development—artistic, technological, agricultural, even spiritual. Somebody also wanted to impress you with the sheer affective power of that object—its ability to involve you in a part of humanity's story, to make the past real in your understanding, to capture your imagination about a world outside your own where people quite different from you created this very thing that you now see as they did, which is now part of your own, inherited culture.

Yes, somebody within the museum has profound respect for that old pot. Respect enough to do extensive research to document its authenticity, understand its origin, and explain its significance. Respect enough to make labels and other learning devices and train docents to provide information about it to you. Respect enough to devise a case to protect the pot yet display it so that you can study and enjoy it. Respect enough even to bring it to your community in a van so that you can visit it conveniently.

Research and *interpretation* are the terms that museum people apply to such work. And research and interpretation are activities that good museums perform. Moreover, many good museums today go out of their way to make their objects and knowledge about them accessible to groups that might otherwise be excluded. In our imaginary van, museum professionals will have installed a ramp or chair lift for people confined to wheelchairs or unable to climb steps. Museum professionals will have provided short, simple labels at eye-level for school-age children, as well as longer, fuller labels, higher up, for adults. And if your area has a sizeable population of speakers of Spanish or other languages besides English, the labels and docent talks will be multilingual. But research, interpretation, and accessible exhibitions are not the only signs of respect for a museum's real things. There is a great deal more.

As you think about it, the other requirements, if one respects collected objects, will become clear. For one thing, respect for an object obviously includes keeping track of it. Consider our imaginary exhibit again. That wonderful ancient pot did not leave its storage area without authorization by the appropriate museum official, who recorded when and where it went, what condition it was in, and when it would be back. In fact, when the museum first received the pot, someone with responsibility for what museum people call *registration* set up a record file on it, manually or in a computer. In that file, one can find out when and from whom the pot was received, what condition it arrived in, whether it came as a gift or a loan (and if a loan, for how long), and what is known about it.

Such records help the museum keep track of its holdings, protect them from loss, make them accessible, and interpret them. A year from now, someone may want to send out the history van again, not with the ancient culture exhibit, but with an exhibit entirely of prehistoric vessels—different kinds from different cultures, with information about changes in techniques of pottery making, in decorative styles and motifs, and in uses of such objects. A search for prehistoric vessels in the museum records will turn up our pot, as well as others, if the documentation is properly and carefully kept and cross-referenced. Or suppose an archaeologist or art historian is studying ancient pottery in museum collections as part of the research needed for a book on that subject. Research projects as well as exhibit developments depend on good museum records, which also keep track of where objects are and, for protective purposes, their condition.

That's another point, of course: respect for an object requires caring about its condition. Our pot will not be available for exhibition or research very long if it gets stolen from the van or damaged while in it. So precautions are taken to protect it. The van will have no windows, or, if there are some, the pot will be exhibited away from them because direct sunlight can harm the vessel and particularly anything painted on it. The van itself will be protected against insects and rodents that might damage its contents. And throughout the van, or at least in the area where objects are displayed, temperature and relative humidity will be controlled to prevent damaging fluctuations in and excessive levels of both. Encasing the pot will also protect it against theft and vandalism, as will the security system for the van as a whole, which may include television monitors, electronic sensing devices, and locks and keys.

Conservation is what museum people call these protective measures. Some museum staffs include scientific conservators. Museums that cannot afford to employ such highly trained professionals full time often contract with conservators.

Actually, if our vessel is truly respected, it will be kept in a protected, secure, and climate-controlled storage area even when it is not in the van, elsewhere on exhibit, or under study by someone. And before the pot is put into the van, someone will have checked to see if it has remained sturdy enough to withstand travel. When it is returned to its home museum, it will be checked again, just as it was when first received, to see whether it needs special treatment to repair damage or arrest deterioration, using methods that conservators judge safe for fragile pottery. Alas, on our planet, everything is more or less subject to deterioration all the time. Respect for museum objects—real things that we value—requires keeping them intact as long as possible.

Research, interpretation, exhibition, registration, conservation, and security—even this is not a complete list of what respect for museum objects requires. However professionally objects have been treated, the pot could still wind up in the city dump when the van returns if, in the interim, the museum has gone broke, its staff lacks appropriate facilities or training, or its board of trustees fails to plan ahead and provide support. Thus, respect also requires fund-raising, strategic planning, adequate physical facilities, and staff training, so that objects in the collections can be cared for properly and used effectively for study, exhibition, and education. Few things are as sad as to learn that an object that has survived centuries of hazards has been ruined by a careless or unsuccessful museum administration.

Museum administration is more demanding in some ways than the administration of regular, for-profit businesses. For one thing, inventory reduction is not anathema for a business but usually a sign of sales success. A museum, however, collects and preserves forever. It may occasionally *deaccession* some object, but usually only if the object turns out to be a fake, legally or ethically belongs to someone else, will more appropriately be part of some other institution's collection, or can be better cared for elsewhere.

The respect we have for the prehistoric pot is different from the respect we have for, say, the word-processing computer on which this book is written. We take care of our personal computers, hoping they will serve at least until we can afford the next, improved version, but that is all. However, if the computer should last so long as to become rare, or serve as an example of early computer development, it may enter a museum collection, as some computers already have done. Then the museum will need to maintain it not only for the present but for future generations. A good museum treats its objects with respect now, but also agrees to do so in perpetuity.

There are variations in the amount of research, interpretation, conservation, and so on that museums give an object, depending on what we respect about it. In interpretation, for example, the extensive kind of descriptive label we use to explain photographs of nineteenth-century mayors in our town might distract from the aesthetic experience we seek when gazing at James Whistler's painting of his mother, about whom biographical information seems less needed. And as we saw from considering the multiple kinds of things that can be studied about our pot, there are many different viewpoints from which to "read" an artifact. There also are different audience perspectives from which to read an artifact, perspectives that need to be respected. For example, not everyone would react in the same way to a display of a Confederate flag.

Also, there are variations in the extent to which museums make real things accessible. Because some valuable museum objects are extremely fragile, museums exhibit them only rarely, or make them accessible only for examination by qualified specialists. Also, some museums use reproductions in exhibits and interpretive programs to save wear and tear on originals, or collect multiple examples of the same kind of object, so that, when one wears out, another will be available. Some museums do not maintain collections of their own at all, but provide opportunities for viewing traveling exhibits from others, or draw on collections of other museums to assemble new exhibits. And museums increasingly use videos, laser technology, and digitized "virtual exhibits" to convey a sense of "real things."

Nonetheless, the real thing underlies all surrogates. And the very act of seeking or accepting an object for a museum collection imputes significance to it. A natural specimen, a work of art, a historical artifact—each has some special value, even if only as an educational tool, or we would not keep it in preference to hundreds of other items. Research may enhance our respect for some object, or changing tastes diminish it. But museums are in the business of assessing the ongoing significance and value for our culture of tangible things, and all the different aspects of museum work are, in essence, logical extensions of respect for the things we decide are worth making a part of humanity's heritage.

The principle of respect is codified in official definitions of museums. The Museum and Library Services Act, which establishes eligibility for grants from the Institute of Museum and Library Services, defines a museum as "a public or private non-profit agency or institution organized on a permanent basis for essentially educational or aesthetic purposes, which, utilizing a professional staff, owns or utilizes tangible objects, cares for them, and exhibits them to the public on a regular basis."

The International Council of Museums defines a museum as "a non-profit making, permanent institution in the service of society and of its development, and open to the public, which acquires, conserves, researches, communicates and exhibits, for purposes of study, education and enjoyment, material evidence of people and their environments."

The American Association of Museums requires that, to be eligible for accreditation, a museum must:

- Be a legally organized not-for-profit institution or part of a not-for-profit institution or government entity

- Be essentially educational in nature

- Have a formally stated mission

- Have one full-time paid professional staff member who has museum knowledge and experience and is delegated authority and allocated financial resources sufficient to operate the museum effectively

- Present regularly scheduled programs and exhibits that use and interpret objects for the public according to accepted standards

- Have a formal and appropriate program of documentation, care, and use of collections and/or tangible objects

- Have a formal and appropriate program of presentation and maintenance of exhibits

Visiting committees that evaluate museums for accreditation use checklists that include questions about governing authority, boards of trustees, staff, membership, finances, facilities, collections, conservation, security, exhibits, programs, overall purposes, and future plans. Meeting these standards will not alone guarantee success, survival, and effective service to one's community, and the standards are sometimes debated and subject to change. What does not change is the basic recognition that much is required if a museum fully implements the principle of respect.

For More Information

The museum accreditation standards mentioned in this chapter, along with much helpful information about the characteristics of an accreditable museum and material for self-study, are found on the website of the American Association of Museums (AAM; www.aam-us.org). Also, two publications about accreditation are available from AAM:

- *Accreditation Resource Kit* (2nd ed., 2001)

- *A Higher Standard: An Accreditation Video* (1996)

For more information on the range of museum responsibilities and activities, nonprofessionals will find help in introductory texts such as the following:

- Burcaw, G. Ellis, *Introduction to Museum Work*, 3rd ed., AltaMira Press, 1997

- Genoways, Hugh H., and Lynne M. Ireland, *Museum Administration: An Introduction*, AltaMira Press, 2003

For readers who decide to go ahead with museum creation, here are more detailed works covering multiple aspects of museum work:

- Ambrose, Timothy, and Crispin Paine, *Museum Basics*, International Council of Museums/Routledge, 1993

- Bryson, John M., and Farnum K. Alston, *Creating and Implementing Your Strategic Plan: A Workbook for Public and Nonprofit Organizations*, Jossey-Bass, 1999

- Edson, Gary, and David Dean, *Handbook for Museums,* Routledge, 1996

- Grinell, Sheila, *A Place for Learning Science: Starting a Science Center and Keeping It Running,* Association of Science-Technology Centers, 2003

- Grinell, Sheila, and Mark St. John, *Vision to Reality: Critical Dimensions in Science Center Development,* 4 vols., Association of Science-Technology Centers, 1993–1996

- Lord, Barry, and Gail Dexter Lord, *The Manual of Museum Planning,* 2nd ed., AltaMira Press, 2000

- Lord, Barry, and Gail Dexter Lord, *The Manual of Museum Management,* AltaMira Press, 1997

- Maher, Mary, ed., *Collective Vision: Starting and Sustaining a Children's Museum: A Comprehensive Guide for New and Existing Institutions,* Association of Youth Museums, 1997

- Maher, Mary, ed., *Capturing the Vision: A Companion Volume,* Association of Youth Museums, 1997

These resource reports available from AAM also provide general information on museum planning and development:

- *Museums and Consultants: Maximizing the Collaboration,* 1996

- *Organizing Your Museum: The Essentials,* 1989

These technical leaflets available from the American Association for State and Local History (www.aaslh.org) also provide general information on museum planning and development:

- *Planning a Local Museum* (78)

- *Some Observations on Establishing Tribal Museums* (134)

A basic bibliography entitled *So You Want to Start a Living History Farm or Museum* is available from the website of the Association for Living History, Farm and Agricultural Museums (www.alhfam.org).

Strong Museum. These children are enjoying interactive exhibits in Rochester's Strong Museum, which includes the National Toy Hall of Fame. Photo courtesy of Strong Museum, Rochester, New York.

2

Help Is All around You

The recognition you now have of all the things it takes to make a good museum may seem rather overwhelming. Fortunately, lots of help is available. Just remember that you did not learn banking, farming, the law, school-teaching, or librarianship overnight, and museum work can be as complicated and demanding as is your business or profession. But expertise is available to you if you know how to find and use it. Here is some help with that.

Assume it is the morning after your community made the decision to start a new museum and appointed you to chair the committee to do it. One of the best things to do first is to check the websites of, and then call, your state's historical society or commission, your state's museum, or your state's museum association. Almost every state has at least one or the other. Explain when you call that you are planning a museum and that you want to do it right.

The first question to ask is what laws and regulations pertain to museums in your state. A local lawyer may be willing to contribute, pro bono publico, some research on nonprofit incorporation, tax-exemption application, and legal responsibilities of public trust institutions such as museums, and it will help to have an attorney on your planning committee from the beginning. Also, the state organization you call may be able to put necessary legal information into your hands or at least identify for you the relevant sections of your state's legal code. States do have laws that pertain to museums, and museums have in fact been sued for not paying attention to them.

Next, you should ask whether the state agency or museum association you are calling, or any other to which it can direct you, has a field-service or museum-consultant program. If you are lucky, you live in a state that respects its heritage enough to support not only a state museum and historical society, but also a field services staff that provides assistance to museums, historical societies, county historical commissions, historic preservation organizations, and the like. Some field services offices put staff members almost continuously on the road to consult directly with museums and heritage organizations, including new ones in planning. Some state historical societies have strong local history programs that work collaboratively with local societies and museums. Some state museums house traveling "museum coordinators" or share specialists, such as conservators, from their in-house staffs. And some state and regional museum associations provide multiple kinds of assistance. You can get a list of field services state by state from the Field Services Alliance on the American Association for State and Local History (AASLH) website (www.aaslh.org/FSA).

If you cannot get an experienced museum person to come out to meet with you about your situation, you might ask whether a professional in one of the state agencies or associations would be willing to let you and others on your planning committee come to him or her for advice. Or someone in a state organization may be able to recommend a private museum consultant, if you can afford to hire outside expertise. Dependable professional consultants are available, although it is wise to check their credentials with museum professionals and previous clients. Also, experienced museum people sometimes are willing to moonlight from their regular jobs by accepting an occasional paid consulting job.

The next question to ask over the phone is, as suggested earlier, which museums already established in your state might be best, in light of the kind and size of museum you have in mind, for you and your planning colleagues to visit. Among other services, your state museum association almost certainly will have a directory of museums in the state and may be willing to identify good examples of museums of the kind you contemplate starting. Also, the national museum directories identified at the end of this book's preface list museums by state.

Behind-the-scenes visits to established museums of the kind you want to create are almost essential for the development of realistic plans, so you may want to extend your search for good models even beyond your state's borders. Regional and national museum associations listed at the end of this chapter can help guide you to good museums to visit for your purposes as well as to other sources of help.

The question to ask last, if at all, during your call to a state agency or association is where to get money for developing your museum. Few if any government agencies and private museum associations at the national, regional, or state levels have grants or other financial assistance for new museums. If you cannot count on a local government or private sources of support within your own community to finance your museum's beginnings, your effort is already in trouble.

By conferring with state organizations and consultants and visiting other museums, you will be finding out, of course, what your costs are likely to be. Then you can explore more knowledgeably the local sources you may need to tap for start-up funds and ongoing financing. More about that in the next chapter.

The first day of your effort is not too soon to check the websites of all relevant state, regional, and national organizations for information on the kinds of assistance and expertise they make available.

The American Association of Museums (AAM), for example, represents museums of all kinds, including planetariums, zoos, and botanical gardens. A wealth of helpful information is available on or through AAM's website (www.aam-us.org), where, among other things, AAM members have access to an Information Center providing guidance on museum operations, standards, "best practices," and emerging issues. Also, AAM maintains a substantial catalogue of publications of use to museums from numerous publishers.

Started in 1906 as a nonprofit organization, AAM has both institutional and individual members, some of whom belong to its standing committees, which include a Trustees Committee and a Small Museums Committee. AAM sponsors workshops and seminars and publishes the magazine *Museum News* and the newsletter *Aviso,* along with many other publications of use to the museum field. AAM's legislative program represents the interests of museums among policy makers in Washington, D.C., seeing that the needs of museums are understood by the Congress, by federal agencies that make grants and administer nonprofit tax policy, and by others of influence.

In addition to the AAM Accreditation Program mentioned earlier, AAM operates a Museum Assessment Program (MAP), through which already established museums that need help in strategic planning can get onsite consultants to provide institutional assessments, collections management assessments, "public dimension" assessments, and governance assessments. The MAP program will not help you plan a new museum, but once yours gets established, MAP can help in its development. The previously mentioned Institute of Museum and Library Services helps museums pay fees for MAP consultations. Information about the MAP program and much else of use to museums may be found on the institute's website (www.imls.gov).

AASLH is another major source of help, particularly for community history museums, which provides useful information on and through AASLH's website (www.aaslh.org) and in the AASLH Book Series of AltaMira Press.

AASLH began in 1940 as a nonprofit association and has both individual and institutional members. Although most AASLH members work in historical societies, historic sites, and archives, as well as in historic houses and history museums, AASLH technical publications have been useful to many kinds of museums. AASLH publishes the magazine *History News* and the newsletter *Dispatch,* along with a technical leaflet series and special reports on topics in museum and historical agency work. AASLH also offers seminars, workshops, awards, and a mentoring program for newcomers. AASLH sponsors a Historic House Task Force "to conduct research and publish best-practice recommendations" of potential help to museums in historic properties, holds workshops on Historic House Museum Issues and Operations, provides a Board Organizer/Orientation Kit of

value to museums that are just starting, and has been developing a performance measurement program for history museums
among other historical organizations.

Other national nonprofit membership associations also provide valuable help to museums of art, science, history, and many
other kinds. So do the six regional museum associations that
cover the United States, and the state museum associations, including some that serve particular parts of states, such as the
Upstate History Alliance and Museum Association of New York,
and some that serve small historical societies with museums,
such as the Bay State Historical League in Massachusetts. In
Canada, the Canadian Museums Association, provincial museum associations, and others offer many kinds of help. Museums dealing with historic properties will find much assistance
available from the National Trust for Historic Preservation
(NTHP) and its national network of regional offices, and many
useful publications from the Preservation Press.

Such national and regional organizations are listed with
contact information at the end of this chapter. Additionally,
AASLH maintains a long list of potentially helpful organizations under "National Resource Links" on its website, and, as
noted earlier in this chapter, its Field Services Alliance page
maintains a list that will help in finding contact information for
state field services. AAM maintains lists of affiliated museum
organizations, regional associations, "professional interest committees and councils" (including the Historic House Museums
Professional Interest Council and committees for Asian/Pacific,
Latino, and Native American museums), and standing professional committees (including the Museum Management Committee and the Small Museum Administrators' Committee). The
National Conference of State Museum Associations maintains a
directory (www.io.com/~tam/smanet) that lists contact information for state museum associations.

Another source of assistance is the growing number of
e-mail discussion groups, through which museum people ask
questions of their peers as they encounter needs and problems.
One such listserv is MuseumL (archive.comlab.ox.ac.uk/other/
museums/museum-1.html). Another, which is valuable for museum documentation information, is MuseDocs (groups.yahoo

.com/group/MuseDocs). Another is a forum for exchanging questions and information about historic house museums (groups .yahoo.com/group/historichousemuseums).

Whether you remain a trustee of your museum, or whether, at least at the outset, you take on some more direct administrative role or day-to-day responsibility, you and your coworkers can use the museum associations to develop your expertise. In addition to helpful publications, these state, regional, and national organizations all have annual meetings, which typically include sessions for people who need basic how-to-do-it information, as well as for more advanced professionals and for museum people in general. Such meetings will give you the opportunity to compare notes with others in comparable museums and share solutions to common problems. Additionally, special seminars and workshops are likely to be available near you from your state historical society or museum association, your regional museum association, or the national museum-service groups. Subjects typically include how to improve fund-raising and public relations, how to give basic care to collections, and how to create effective exhibits.

And who knows?—if you, yourself, get hooked on museum work, you may decide to turn the car dealership over to Junior, give up your garden club, or abandon golf as an insufficiently challenging occupation for a retired military officer, and pursue a new career. Then you will want to think about taking short-term training courses for overall development of museum skills, such as the Winedale Museum Seminar on Administration and Interpretation sponsored by the University of Texas Center for American History, the annual Seminar for Historical Administration cosponsored by AAM, AASLH, Colonial Williamsburg, the Indiana Historical Society, the National Park Service, and NTHP, or the Museum Management Institute sponsored by the Getty Leadership Institute in California.

Many universities now offer formal degree programs for people who wish to pursue careers in museums. In addition to museum studies courses, "public history" programs, which prepare higher-education graduates for many kinds of historical work besides teaching, including museum work, have grown in numbers and popularity. AASLH, AAM, the National Council on Public History, and other associations can guide you to lists of such programs, as well as to standards for evaluating them. It is useful to know about these academic programs even if you, yourself, will do no more than judge the credentials of museum professionals whom you may want to hire. But some universities are also sources of publications, conferences, and programs of help in museum work generally. Some make students available to help museums as interns or undertake activities for museums as class projects. Check at universities near you about programs they may have in museum studies and public history.

You now have a good idea of what you are getting into and are aware of what kind of help is available. As you think about moving forward, it is time to ask: Can you afford it?

For More Information

Depending on what kind of museum you are starting, some of the following organizations can help if you check their websites and contact them for information about their publications, programs, and services. The following contact information is as of the time of this writing and may change, particularly for organizations that are administered by changing, elected officers rather than from a permanent headquarters. If you do not find an organization listed here by using the following contact information, check with AAM, AASLH, or NTHP.

National Organizations

These organizations provide national representation, varied services, and helpful publications to the kinds of museums and museum constituencies described in their titles. Identify the organizations in this list whose names seem most pertinent to your needs and check their websites for offerings of use to you.

American Arts Alliance
1112 16th Street, NW, Suite 400
Washington, DC 20036
(202) 833-2787
www.americanartsalliance.org

American Association for Museum Volunteers
c/o Liz Gumerman, Museum of Northern Arizona
3101 N. Fort Valley Road
Flagstaff, AZ 86001
(928) 774-5213
www.aamv.org

American Association for State and Local History
1717 Church Street
Nashville, TN 37203
(615) 320-3203
www.aaslh.org

American Association of Botanical Gardens and Arboreta
100 West 10th Street, Suite 614
Wilmington, DE 19801
(302) 655-7100
www.aabga.org

American Association of Museums
1575 Eye Street, NW, Suite 400
Washington, DC 20005
(202) 289-1818
www.aam-us.org

American Federation of Arts
41 E. 65th Street
New York, NY 10021
(212) 861-2487 or (800) 232-0270
www.afaweb.org

American Indian Museums Program
sponsored by AASLH, 1717 Church Street
Nashville, TN 37203
(615) 320-3203
www.aaslh.org/beta/aaslh/aimp.htm

American Institute for Conservation of Historic and Artistic Works
1717 K Street, NW, Suite 200
Washington, DC 20006
(202) 452-9545
http://aic.stanford.edu

American Zoo and Aquarium Association
8403 Colesville Road, Suite 710
Silver Spring, MD 20910
(301) 562-0777
www.aza.org

Association for Living History, Farm and Agricultural
  Museums
c/o Steve Miller, Landis Valley Museum
2451 Kissel Hill Road
Lancaster, PA 17601
(717) 581-0595 or (717) 569-0401
www.alhfam.org

Association of African American Museums
c/o National Afro-American Museum and Cultural Center
PO Box 578
1350 Brush Row Road
Wilberforce, OH 45384
(937) 376-4611
www.blackmuseums.org

Association of Art Museum Directors
41 E. 65th Street
New York, NY 10021
(212) 249-4423
www.aamd.org

Association of Children's Museums
1300 L Street, NW, Suite 975
Washington, DC 20005
(202) 898-1080
www.childrensmuseums.org

Association of College and University Museums and
  Galleries
c/o Lisa Tremper Hanover, Berman Museum of Art,
  Ursinus College
601 East Main Street
Collegeville, PA 19426
(610) 409-3500
www.acumg.org

Association of Railway Museums
PO Box 370
Tujunga, CA 91043
(818) 951-9151
www.railwaymuseums.org

Association of Science Museum Directors
c/o St. Louis Science Center
5050 Oakland Avenue
St. Louis, MO 63110
(314) 289-4474

Association of Science-Technology Centers
1025 Vermont Avenue, NW, Suite 500
Washington, DC 20005
(202) 783-7200
www.astc.org

Canadian Museums Association
280 Metcalfe Street, Suite 400
Ottawa, Ontario K2P 1R7, Canada
(613) 567-0099
www.museums.ca

Council for Museum Anthropology
American Anthropological Association
4350 North Fairfax Drive, Suite 640
Arlington, VA 22203-1621
(703) 528-1902
www.nmnh.si.edu/cma

Council of American Jewish Museums
330 7th Avenue, 21st Floor
New York, NY 10001
(212) 629-0500
www.jewishculture.org/museums/museums.html

Council of American Maritime Museums
c/o Thomas R. Wilcox Jr., Maine Maritime Museum
243 Washington Street

Bath, ME 04530
(207) 443-1316
www.councilofamericanmaritimemuseums.org

Heritage Preservation
1625 K Street, NW, Suite 700
Washington, DC 20006
(202) 634-1422
www.heritagepreservation.org

International Association of Museum Facility Administrators
c/o High Museum of Art
1280 Peachtree Road, NE
Atlanta, GA 30309
(404) 733-4407
www.iamfa.org

International Association of Sports Museums and Halls of Fame
180 N. LaSalle Street, Suite 1822
Chicago, IL 60601
(312) 551-0810
www.sportshalls.com

International Council of Museums: http://icom.museums
- U.S. ICOM Committee
  AAM ICOM, American Association of Museums
  1575 Eye Street, NW, Suite 400
  Washington, DC 20005
  (202) 218-7680
  http://usa.icom.museums
- Canada ICOM Committee
  ICOM Museums-Musées Canada
  280 Metcalfe Street, Suite 400
  Ottawa, Ontario K2P 1R7, Canada
  (613) 567-0099
  http://canada.icom.museums

International Museum Theatre Alliance
c/o Jonathan Ellers, Central Park Wildlife Center

830 5th Avenue
New York, NY 10021
(212) 439-6542
www.mos.org/imtal

Museum Computer Network
232-329 March Road, Box 11
Ottawa, Ontario K2K 2E1, Canada
(613) 254-9772
www.mcn.edu

Museum Store Association
4100 E. Mississippi Avenue, Suite 800
Denver, CO 80246
(303) 504-9223
www.museumdistrict.com

Museum Studies Reference Library
National Museum of Natural History, Room 27
10th Street and Constitution Avenue, NW
Washington, DC 20013
Mailing Address: Smithsonian Institution Libraries
PO Box 37012
NHB 27, MRC 154
Washington, DC 20013
(202) 357-2139
www.sil.si.edu/libraries/mrc-hp.htm

Museum Trustee Association
2025 M Street, NW, Suite 800
Washington, DC 20036
(202) 367-1180
www.mta-hq.org

National Association for Interpretation
PO Box 2246
Fort Collins, CO 80522
(970) 484-8283
www.interpnet.com

National Association of Museum Exhibition
This is the Standing Professional Committee on Exhibition of

AAM and maintains a virtual office at its website www.n-a-m-e.org
Or contact Kristine Hastreiter at (508) 212-4415

National Council on Public History
327 Cavanaugh Hall
IUPUI
425 University Boulevard
Indianapolis, IN 46202
(317) 274-2716
www.ncph.org

National Park Service Library Information Center
c/o San Francisco Maritime National Historical Park
Lower Ft. Mason, Building E, 2nd Floor
San Francisco, CA 94123
(510) 758-3975
www.library.nps.gov

(You may also explore assistance possibilities from the National
    Park Service by contacting the cultural resource
    management/interpretive office at a national park near you)

National Trust for Historic Preservation
1785 Massachusetts Avenue, NW
Washington, DC 20036
(202) 588-6000
www.nationaltrust.org

Natural Science Collections Alliance
1725 K Street, NW, Suite 601
Washington, DC 20006
(202) 835-9050
www.nscalliance.org

Oral History Association
oha@dickinson.edu
www.dickinson.edu/oha

Smithsonian Institution Traveling Exhibition Services
PO Box 37012
1100 Jefferson Davis Drive, SW, Suite 3146
Washington, DC 20013

(202) 633-3168

www.sites.si.edu

Society for American Archaeology
900 2nd Street, NE, #12
Washington, DC 20002
(202) 789-8200
www.saa.org

Society for the Preservation of Natural History Collections
c/o Lisa Palmer
PO Box 797
Washington, DC 20044
www.spnhc.org

Society of American Archivists
527 South Wells Street, 5th Floor
Chicago, IL 60607
(312) 922-0140
www.archivists.org

Society of Architectural Historians
1365 N. Astor Street
Chicago, IL 60610
(312) 573-1365
www.sah.org

U.S. Regional Museum Organizations

These organizations can help developing museums of many
kinds. Call or check the website of the organization for your region to see how it can help with your needs.

Association of Midwest Museums
(Illinois, Indiana, Iowa, Michigan, Minnesota, Missouri, Ohio,
    and Wisconsin)
PO Box 11940
St. Louis, MO 63112
(314) 454-3110
www.midwestmuseums.org

Mid-Atlantic Association of Museums
(Delaware, Maryland, New Jersey, New York, Pennsylvania,
and District of Columbia)
800 E. Lombard Street
Baltimore, MD 21202
(410) 223-1194
www.midatlanticmuseums.org

Mountain-Plains Museum Association
(Colorado, Kansas, Montana, Nebraska, New Mexico, North
Dakota, Oklahoma, South Dakota, Texas, and Wyoming)
7110 West David Drive
Littleton, CO 80128
(303) 979-9358
www.mountplainsmuseums.org

New England Museums Association
(Connecticut, Maine, Massachusetts, New Hampshire, Rhode
Island, and Vermont)
22 Mill Street, Suite 409
Arlington, MA 02476
(781) 641-0013
www.nemanet.org

Southeastern Museums Conference
(Alabama, Arkansas, Florida, Georgia, Kentucky, Louisiana,
Mississippi, North Carolina, South Carolina, Tennessee,
Virginia, West Virginia, Puerto Rico, and Virgin Islands)
PO Box 9003
Atlanta, GA 31106
(404) 378-3153
www.semcdirect.net

Western Museums Conference
(Alaska, Arizona, California, Hawaii, Idaho, Nevada, Oregon,
Utah, Washington, and British Columbia)
2960 San Pablo Avenue
Berkeley, CA 94702
(510) 665-0700
www.westmuse.org

Regional Offices of the National Trust for Historic Preservation

These offices can help museums that are planning to preserve and use historic houses and other historic properties. Call or check the website of the office for your region.

Midwest Office
(Illinois, Indiana, Iowa, Michigan, Minnesota, Missouri, Ohio, and Wisconsin)
53 W. Jackson Boulevard, Suite 350
Chicago IL 60604
(312) 939-5547
www.nthp.org/about_the_trust/regional/midwest.html

Mountains/Plains Office
(Colorado, Kansas, Montana, Nebraska, North Dakota, South Dakota, Utah, and Wyoming)
535 16th Street, Suite 750
Denver, CO 80202
(303) 623-1504
www.nthp.org/about_the_trust/regional/mountain.html

Northeast Office
(Connecticut, Delaware, Maine, Massachusetts, New Hampshire, New Jersey, New York, Pennsylvania, Rhode Island, and Vermont; also, this region has a field office in Philadelphia and "circuit riders" in Connecticut and Vermont)
Seven Faneuil Hall, Marketplace
Boston, MA 02109
(617) 523-0885
www.nthp.org/about_the_trust/regional/northeast.html

Southern Office
(Alabama, District of Columbia, Florida, Georgia, Kentucky, Louisiana, Maryland, Mississippi, North Carolina, Puerto Rico, South Carolina, Tennessee, Virginia, Virgin Islands, and West Virginia; also, this region has a field office in Washington, D.C., for preservation activities in Maryland, Virginia, West Virginia, and the District of Columbia)

456 King Street
Charleston, SC 29403
(843) 722-8552
www.nthp.org/about_the_trust/regional/southern.html

Southwest Office
(Arkansas, New Mexico, Oklahoma, and Texas)
500 Main Street, Suite 1030
Fort Worth, TX 76102
(817) 332-4398
www.nthp.org/about_the_trust/regional/southwest.html

Western Office
(Alaska, Arizona, California, Hawaii, Idaho, Nevada, Oregon,
    and Washington)
8 California Street, Suite 400
San Francisco, CA 94111
(415) 956-0610
www.nthp.org/about_the_trust/regional/western.html

Regional Conservation Centers (Members of the Regional Alliance for Preservation)

These organizations can help with the care of collections. Particularly if you have concerns about the condition of objects available for your museum, call or check the website of the center nearest you.

Amigos Preservation Service
Amigos Library Services, Inc.
14400 Midway Road
Dallas, TX 75244
(972) 851-8000 or (800) 843-8482
www.amigos.org

Balboa Art Conservation Center
PO Box 3755
San Diego, CA 92163
(619) 236-9702

The Conservation Center for Art and Historic Artifacts
265 South 23rd Street
Philadelphia, PA 19103
(215) 545-0613
www.ccaha.org

Gerald R. Ford Conservation Center
1326 South 32nd Street
Omaha, NE 68105
www.nebraskahistory.org/fordcenter

Intermuseum Conservation Association
2915 Detroit Avenue
Cleveland, OH 44113
(216) 658-8700
www.oberlin/edu/~ica

National Park Service Division of Conservation, Harpers Ferry
     Center
Division of Conservation
PO Box 50
Harpers Ferry, WV 25425
(304) 535-6228
www.nps.gov/hfc/conservation

Northeast Document Conservation Center
100 Brickstone Square
Andover, MA 01810
(978) 470-1010
www.nedcc.org

Peebles Island Resource Center, New York State Office of Parks,
     Recreation, and Historic Preservation
PO Box 219
Waterford, NY 12188
(518) 237-8643
www.nysparks.com/hist/history.html

The Southeastern Library Network, Inc., Preservation Services
1438 West Peachtree Street, NW, Suite 200
Atlanta, GA 30309
www.solinet.net

The Straus Center for Conservation
Harvard University Art Museums
32 Quincy Street
Cambridge, MA 02138
(617) 495-2392
www.artmuseums.harvard.edu

The Textile Conservation Center
American Textile History Museum
491 Dutton Street
Lowell, MA 01854
(978) 441-1198
www.athm.org

The Textile Conservation Workshop
Main Street
South Salem, NY 10590
(914) 763-5805

The Upper Midwest Conservation Association
Minneapolis Institute of Arts
2400 3rd Avenue South
Minneapolis, MN 55404
(612) 870-3120
www.preserveart.org

Williamstown Art Conservation Center
225 South Street
Williamstown, MA 01267
(413) 458-5741
www.williamstownart.org

Drayton Hall. The 260-year history of this grand colonial mansion near Charleston, South Carolina, is interpreted by the National Trust for Historic Preservation. Photo by Ron Blunt. Courtesy of the National Trust for Historic Preservation.

3

Support Is the First Consideration

Had this book been revised in the 1990s, much of what its first edition said about financing museums could have remained unchanged. But then came a precipitous fall in the stock market, which eroded the value and earnings of invested endowment funds for those museums that had such assets, and reduced as well the stock market income that philanthropic foundations and individual donors could contribute to museums. As the overall economy struggled, government revenues from income and sales taxes declined, forcing substantial cuts in budgets of museums supported by state and local governments. Even some long-established and well-run museums faced severe economic difficulties. All this is to say that museums cannot take financial support for granted. And anyone considering a new museum will be wise to assess its potential support before ever making a commitment.

Even before setting your museum's statement of purpose in stone, analyze the prospects for support for the kind of museum you have in mind. If the public is not interested in what your museum will be and do, and if no one in your community will contribute the necessary financial backing, you could have marvelous collections and a magnificent building without being able to maintain either. And if your nonprofit museum organization has accepted responsibility for a collection or a building that it cannot afford to maintain, you could be in danger of violating the public trust laws of your state.

Museums need to consider the interests and potential size of their targeted audiences long before opening their doors. For whom—for what "audience"—are you planning a museum? Residents of your town, your county, your region, or beyond? Do you hope to attract tourists as well? Either way, do you want to reach families, students, or senior citizens? Or is yours to be a college museum, serving students and faculty? Or a military museum providing components of personnel training? Or a museum for members of a particular ethnic, professional, or special-interest group? What interests the kind of visitors and program participants you want? How will you attract them? What will be the marketing costs of analyzing and attracting these desired groups?

A word of caution about tourists. Some museums depend on them for revenue and market heavily and effectively to draw them, financially benefiting local communities by doing so. But unless your museum can offer something of exceptional interest to a wide public, you will find it hard to depend on tourism. A strong base of local support is the best prospect for a museum's perpetual financing.

If you can afford professional help, a competent development firm will know how to analyze potential support for your museum as well as how to raise money for it. Either way, many things need consideration as you assess your financial requirements and prospects.

First, try to identify all the costs you will need to cover. Some expenses will be more or less fixed, necessary costs of doing anything at all. General overhead expenses are in this category: costs of such things as facility maintenance (heat, air conditioning, electricity, and security); of basic personnel (at least the director's salary and fringe benefits, and funds for recruiting, training, and rewarding volunteers); of office equipment, supplies, and services (computers, software, telephone, and postage); and of routine collections care. Also, you may have to contract for things such as trash hauling, roof repairing, and event catering. Other expenses will be incurred when special projects are undertaken, such as the costs of designing and constructing an exhibit, of conducting a particular "outreach" activity, of mailing publicity for a special promotion, or of printing a new publication or brochure. Document D at the back of this book provides a typical list of line items in museum budgets. The costs of adapting a building or acquiring a collection are only the start of a museum's expenses.

After determining your likely ongoing and upfront financial needs, consider then where you might get support for your overall budget or parts of it. If you are planning a museum because you have already been offered a collection, a building, or both, see if whoever made the offer—perhaps a wealthy private donor or some special group—would also contribute an endowment fund to cover costs of care and exhibition of the collection or rehabilitation and maintenance of the building. Or if the original donor has given to the limit, would someone else provide an endowment fund, or a challenge grant that others could be asked to match to create an endowment? An endowment fund is a sum of money for permanent investment, earning annual interest that, in whole or part, may be used to support a museum's ongoing operations.

If no endowment fund is available or if the interest from one will not cover all of your probable expenses, then you may need to ask whether your city, county, or some other unit of government will appropriate money on a regular basis from tax or bond revenues to support your museum.

If neither endowment funds nor public appropriations will be available or adequate in amount, then private fund-raising of various kinds will be necessary. Can you recruit philanthropists in your community to serve on your museum's board of trustees—persons who are willing to contribute funds themselves every year, persuade others to contribute, or both? Almost every museum depends to some extent on financial assistance from board members, even if it has other resources. Although some board members may contribute services rather than cash, taking responsibility for the financial health of an organization is a board duty. Staff can help organize fund-raising and directors can help make pitches, but ensuring the financing of the museum is the board's responsibility and board members must take the leadership in raising funds, which includes lobbying to maintain them if contributions come from government bodies.

Along with board contributions, can you fill out your budget from the proceeds of some special, annual fund-raising event? In analyzing this option, take a close look at other nonprofit cultural organizations in your community. How many already support themselves through private fund-raising? How well are they doing? If already established organizations are struggling to raise money, filling the community calendar with fund-raising events, or competing for the allegiance of wealthy individuals, how much chance will your museum have at a piece of the available pie?

Does the symphony have an annual street fair with food, music, and dancing? Does the historic preservation group organize profit-making tours, travel opportunities, and a lecture series? Does the public television station have an antique auction in addition to on-air pledge campaigns? Do youth groups, homeless shelters, or health organizations sponsor benefit performances by popular entertainers? Do civic clubs sell raffle tickets? And do veterans' organizations sell lapel flowers? Is the college about to launch another capital-fund drive? If all these cultural, educational, and social service organizations are not already exhausting the capacity for private giving in your community, what kind of special fund-raising device can you use for the museum?

Also, how much of your budget can you hope to cover from admission fees? Many museums ask visitors to pay entrance fees, which vary greatly in amount, depending on the size and drawing power of the museum. It will be useful to consult with museums in your area of the size and kind you are considering to see what their experience has made them feel able to charge. Some museums give discounts to students, senior citizens, and tour groups, and some charge lesser fees on days when visitation is otherwise likely to be light. Some charge more for special exhibits. Also, museums often charge fees for special events and programs, and many museums negotiate revenue-generating contracts with public schools to provide special tours and programs as part of educational curricula. If your museum is going to receive a significant part of its support from governmental agencies, they may take the view that citizens should be able to visit tax-supported institutions at low cost or none. If you can charge, you might fruitfully do market research by asking groups of potential visitors about the size of fees they would expect or be willing to pay.

Many museums also offer annual memberships, which generally cost more than visitor fees and provide special benefits. These may include free or discounted passes, newsletters or other publications for members only, discounts on museum store purchases, previews of exhibits, and other special events. Again, consulting established museums about membership programs can be useful. Offering memberships can involve individuals more fully with the museum and give the museum an interested base of donor prospects to cultivate. But one must be careful that membership benefits do not cost the museum more than the resulting income.

Museums have become aggressive in pursuing opportunities for earned income. Included are publications, such as exhibit catalogs, that museums sell. Large museums commonly contain cafes or cafeterias that may return a profit. And museum stores have become popular with the public. These range from the substantial merchandising operations of large museums, which sell through catalogs as well as on their premises, to next-to-the-exit cubicles in which small museums offer a few publications and souvenirs for sale. Care must be taken that earned income from museum sales does not jeopardize the tax-exempt status of the overall institution. The Museum Stores Association can provide guidance on tax rules as well as on other facets of museum merchandizing. Some historic house museums add to their revenue by renting certain areas in their facilities or grounds for weddings, parties, and other nonmuseum events. Helpful revenues may be generated, but a museum must first assure itself that outsiders' events can be accommodated without damage to the historic property or its collections.

Finally, museums commonly seek support in the form of in-kind rather than cash contributions. Will a local lawyer and a local accountant act as friends of the museum by handling its legal and bookkeeping needs without charge or at reduced rates? Will lumber yards and hardware dealers donate construction materials for exhibits or provide them at cost? Will your city or county help at least by providing custodial and security services for the museum? Will landscaping firms take care of, or garden clubs make special projects of, the museum's grounds? And most important, will you be able to recruit a cadre of regular and capable volunteers? Almost no museum operates entirely with paid staff. Many museums enlist volunteers to guide visitors, assist with publicity and fund-raising, help with research and collections inventories, or whatever else is needed for which competent persons will volunteer.

Once you have considered what your upfront and continuing costs may be and which sources of revenue are open to you, then you need to test the conclusions you have reached and the assumptions on which they are based. You can do that by interviewing some of the kinds of people whose support you will need—local philanthropists, business leaders, elected officials, officers of civic clubs, newspaper publishers, broadcast executives, and other influential citizens—to see if they share your enthusiasm and encourage you to seek community support. You can also ask potential visitors, individually, in focus groups, or through surveys, to indicate how supportive they might be of your museum.

At the outset, some museums have called community meetings to assess support. To such a meeting, you could invite anyone interested in art, science, history, or whatever you envision for the focus of your museum to come hear your plans and discuss their pros and cons. Invitations may be extended at large, through news media and posters in store windows, and through special mailings to and appearances before service clubs and other community groups. If you get the word out well in advance and make the meeting interesting, the size of the turnout may itself tell you much about the prospects for your museum. Among other things, the turnout may help you analyze your chances for supporting the museum at least in part with admission charges and membership dues.

In addition to startup expenses and ongoing operating costs, your plan needs to provide for seeking donors for special one-time activities. Typically, as a museum plans a special exhibit, it requests money from foundations, corporations, or individual donors for whom an exhibit may have special interest. Persons experienced with this kind of fund-raising in other arenas will be aware that extensive research is needed to identify such prospects, along with other kinds of donors. In fact, you will need to raise funds even for fund-raising; that is, your budget will need to cover costs of consultants, staff time, and materials such as brochures that are needed in fund-raising.

Ideally, if like most museums you must depend on multiple revenue sources, your plan and annual budgets will identify which of those sources can realistically be expected to cover each particular kind of cost. Will county tax appropriations pay for staff salaries and fringe benefits? Will the city government provide utilities, maintenance, and security for the museum's building? Will membership dues or admission charges take care of other operating costs? Will special exhibits and projects with heavy costs be undertaken only if grants from corporations, foundations, or individual donors are secured specifically for them? Will acquisitions each year depend on the success of an annual fund-raising event? Will additional fund-raising be necessary to build an endowment fund that can generate interest income for each year's budget? Will a special capital-fund drive be needed for a building renovation or expansion?

Business executives on your board, in addition to giving and raising money, may be able to contribute further to your museum's financial well-being from their experience in assessing financial risks, weighing alternative investment options, estimating and controlling costs, evaluating alternative sources of supplies, judging the cost-effectiveness of operations and proposals, and maintaining financial controls. Your goal, of course, is not to make a financial profit, like a successful business, but to produce a cultural payoff for your community on its investment in the museum. Nonetheless, a museum is like a business in being unable to operate very long at a financial loss. Unless some wealthy individual is willing to underwrite your losses every year, good business judgment will be as necessary for your museum as for the local construction company or car dealership.

Good business includes initial and continual marketing research, so that you keep track of the interests of communities you wish to attract and of how they are reacting to your museum. A museum with a defined social mission cannot heedlessly adjust to market whims, but it can develop special mission-related programming for particular audiences, and it can advertise itself in ways that speak to audiences' interests and needs. Keeping in meaningful touch with the communities you serve will be essential. And if your market research at the outset brings to light substantial indifference within the audiences you had hoped to serve and looked to for support, you will be wise to consider alternatives, such as those described in the next chapter.

For More Information

Concerning financial planning, the following are useful:

- American Association of Museums (AAM), *Slaying the Financial Dragon: Strategies for Museums*, AAM, 2003

- Dierking, Lynn D., and Wendy Pollock, *Questioning Assumptions: An Introduction to Front-End Studies in Museums*, Association of Science-Technology Centers, 1998

- Graham, Christine, *Keep the Money Coming: A Step-by-Step Strategic Guide to Annual Fundraising*, Pineapple Press, 2001

- Howe, Fisher, *The Board Member's Guide to Fund Raising: What Every Trustee Needs to Know about Raising Money*, Jossey-Bass, 1991

- Kotler, Neil, and Philip Kotler, *Museum Strategy and Marketing: Designing Missions, Building Audiences, Generating Revenue and Resources*, Jossey-Bass, 1998

- Rosso, Henry A., and Associates, *Achieving Excellence in Fund Raising: A Comprehensive Guide to Principles, Strategies, and Methods*, Jossey-Bass, 1991

- Schaff, Terry, and Doug Schaff, *The Fundraising Planner: A Working Model for Raising the Dollars You Need*, Jossey-Bass, 1999

The following technical leaflets published by the American Association for State and Local History (AASLH) are also pertinent to museum financing:

- *Financing Your History Organization: Setting Goals* (106)
- *Fundraising for the Small Museum* (209)
- *Recruiting Members for Your Historical Society* (37)

On the financial management of museums, the following are useful:

- Dropkin, Murray, and Allyson Hayden, *The Cash Flow Management Book for Nonprofits: A Step-by-Step Guide for Managers, Consultants, and Boards,* Jossey-Bass, 2001
- Dropkin, Murray, and Bill LaTouche, *The Budget-Building Book for Nonprofits: A Step-by-Step Guide for Managers and Boards,* Jossey-Bass, 1998
- Gross, Malvern J., Jr., et al., *Financial and Accounting Guide for Not-for-Profit Organizations,* 6th ed., John Wiley and Sons, 2000
- McLaughlin, Tom, *Presenting Nonprofit Financials: An Overview of Board Fiduciary Responsibility,* BoardSource, 2001
- Ruppel, Warren, *Not-for-Profit Accounting Made Easy,* John Wiley and Sons, 2002

Also, the following technical leaflets from AASLH pertain to financial management:

- *Financial Management for the Local Historical Society* (164)
- *Forming a Purchasing Cooperative* (190)
- *The Gift of History, Using the Gift of History to Promote Your Organization* (208)
- *Preparing an Earned Income Strategy* (165)
- *Site Analysis for Tourism Potential* (172)

On museum store development and management, the following may be useful:

- Museum Store Association, *The New Store Workbook: MSA's Guide to the Essential Steps from Business Plan to Opening Day*, Museum Store Association, 2001 (the Museum Store Association offers more specialized publications as well through its website, www.museumdistrict.com)
- Theobald, Mary Miley, *Museum Store Management*, AASLH/AltaMira Press, 2000
- Virtue, Mary, and Jane Delgado, *The Museum Shop Workbook*, The African American and Latino Art Museum Working Group, 1995

Also, the following technical leaflet from AASLH pertains to earned revenue:

- *Selling History: A Practical Primer on Museum Product Development and Licensing* (205)

On museum marketing and public relations, the following are useful:

- Adams, G. Donald, *Museum Public Relations*, AASLH/AltaMira Press, 1983
- Hooper-Greenhill, Eilean, *Museums and Their Visitors*, Routledge, 1994
- McLean, Fiona, *Marketing the Museum*, Routledge, 1997
- Runyard, Sue, and Ylva French, *Marketing and Public Relations Handbook for Museums, Galleries, and Heritage Attractions*, AltaMira Press, 2000

Also, the following resource reports from AAM pertain to marketing and public relations:

- AAM, *Taking Charge of Your Museum's Public Relations Destiny*, 1990

- Hall, Jason, *How to Be Your Museum's Best Advocate,* 1994
- Korn, Randi, and Laurie Sowd, *Visitor Surveys: A User's Manual,* 1990

Also, the following technical leaflets and video from AASLH pertain to marketing and public relations:

- *Effective Public Relations: Communicating Your Image* (3)
- *Working Effectively with the Press* (124)
- *Marketing and Promoting Interpretive Programs* (video 478VT)

Lower East Side Tenement Museum. The Gumpertz Kitchen is exhibited in the Lower East Side Tenement Museum, a property of the National Trust for Historic Preservation, which interprets immigration history. Photo by Carol Highsmith. Courtesy of the National Trust for Historic Preservation.

4

And If You Don't Want to Do All That?

Once again, are you starting or expanding a museum to house a collection that you would like to present to the public, or a collection that has been given to your historical society, or collections that your historical society, art league, or nature group has accumulated that have outgrown the storage and display areas you have at present? In short, are you developing a museum because you have a collection that should be in one?

There is no law that says it has to be in a new museum, or even in one of your own.

You may save yourself a lot of trouble by checking first to see if an existing museum in your area already has collections like yours. If so, and you start a new museum, competition for visitors and money is likely to keep both of you weak, while making it harder to give your collection proper care and attractive exhibition. But if the already established museum would be augmented by your collection, and if it has the staff, facilities, and financing to give your collection good care, you might do yourself and the existing museum a favor by seeing if it would be interested in the donation of your collection.

Or you might find the best home for your collection by looking far beyond your own area. The previously identified directories compiled by the American Association of Museums (AAM) and the American Association for State and Local History (AASLH) can help you find established museums that specialize in the kind of works of art, historical artifacts, or scientific specimens that you have collected or that your organization has received. Your antique furniture, early-day farm implements, or paintings by regional artists may be especially valued by museums that have long cared for such things. War memorabilia, for example, may interest the many museums maintained by the U.S. Army, Air Force, Navy, Marine Corps, and Coast Guard. You may be able to help other museums fill gaps, making their collections more representative and complete. Assuming there are no legal restrictions on disposal of the collection you possess, you could negotiate a gift that would ensure perpetual care for your collection instead of setting up a duplicate museum.

Even if no potentially competing museum already exists in your area, an alternative to the work and expense of starting your own is to consolidate efforts with others. That is, maybe others in your region have collections for which they, too, are considering new museums, or would be willing to expand the collection range and service area of an existing museum. You might be able to enlist enough cooperation to organize a regional museum whose board of directors would represent multiple communities and whose programs would include traveling exhibits and other museum programs reaching into your town and county as well as others. Such a regional museum could have a better chance of securing a strong financial base, which would ensure long-term security for your collection while also providing museum experiences for people in your community among others in the area. Those are some options, if your motive for museum building is to house collections.

But what if you are that chamber of commerce person whose motive for a new museum is to attract money-spending tourists to your community? Clearly, you still must consider what you have—sites, buildings, and collections—that will attract tourists. Remember, if you have nothing of exceptional interest to a wide public, you are not likely to draw tourists away from other attractions. But if you have such collections, if you have figured accurately what it costs to create a truly attractive museum and effectively advertise it to tourists, and if you are sure that the financial return to your community will cover and justify such costs, then creating a museum can be commendable. There are, however, easier ways to use a community's heritage to attract visitors.

An annual festival is one way. Many communities draw thousands of visitors to special commemorations of historical events, observances of the anniversaries of famous persons, demonstrations of regional arts and crafts, or celebrations of something for which a locality is notable, such as an agricultural or industrial product. Some communities draw numerous visitors by offering candlelight tours of privately owned historic houses. Developing attractive events takes imagination and research but not the continuous commitment, fund-raising, and legal responsibility that a museum requires.

What if you are one of those who saved a historic building in your community as a prospect for a museum? This museum might not simply house exhibits but become one; that is, the old building itself is what people would come to see, along with furnishings it once contained, if you are lucky enough to have them, or with furnishings like those it probably had, if you are lucky enough to have documentation of how it was furnished. But if not, there are many other useful things that you can do instead with a fine historic house, an old school, a train station, or some other significant structure.

Adaptive use of old structures is common and condoned by historic preservationists, at least under certain conditions. These can be explained to you by your local historic preservation group, your city's historical commission, or your state's historic preservation office. The preservation office might appear under the name of your state's historical society or of a government department such as parks or conservation. The federal government helps to finance state historic preservation offices, whose staffs advise citizens about historic preservation standards, legal restrictions, tax benefits, and sources of financial aid. Also, such advice is available from your region's office of the National Trust for Historic Preservation (whose regional offices are listed at the end of chapter 2).

Adaptive use of a building essentially means that you keep the building alive and useful in your community by adapting it from its original purpose to some new function, such as rehabilitating a downtown waterfront warehouse for shops and restaurants or turning a stately old residence into attractive office space. Some historical societies have adaptively used abandoned railway depots for offices for themselves with storage facilities and meeting rooms.

Such uses may require less extensive—and even less expensive—alteration in the interiors of historic buildings than refitting their interiors for secure, climate-controlled care of museum collections. The old county courthouse may have a wonderful open atrium for exhibits, but that does not make it easy or cheap to heat and cool uniformly, to rewire for security devices, to replumb for a conservation lab, or to reequip with light fixtures and window treatments that help protect collections. You could just as well preserve the grand old building by rehabilitating it for rent-paying office use. Thus, rather than becoming an expensive rehabilitation for museum purposes, a properly preserved historic building adapted for commercial use could become a source of income for a cultural or community organization. Nonprofit cultural and educational organizations do not necessarily surrender their tax-exempt status by such income-generating activities; they can and do lease space to others in historic properties.

There are other alternatives if you are the park department official who has been asked to use an old building on a historic site for museum exhibits. You already know that without collections you cannot do permanent exhibits. But even if you do have collections, that old building may not be adequate for exhibiting, recording, storing, conserving, and securing them. Moreover, museum exhibits are not necessarily the best way to explain a site, which, after all, is your real goal. Less complicated, less expensive methods can be used to explain the significance of a place to visitors and help them get a feeling for what happened there.

Do you recall, for example, visiting a Civil War battlefield at which the National Park Service showed a film or slide show about the site or used lines of lights in a relief map to explain the flow of a battle, and then sent you out with an interpretive brochure for a walking tour, along which you found historical markers to explain what happened at certain points? A few markers and inexpensive, illustrated pamphlets can be excellent ways to interpret a small site for visitors. Tour pamphlets can be reprinted and markers replaced without the kind of perpetual care needed for museum collections and are easier to come by than genuine Civil War cannons or Revolutionary-era army uniforms. Also, digital audiovisual and interactive technologies now make possible wonderfully effective presentations of historical information, nature lore, and aesthetic insight, without the need to care for permanent museum collections.

Finally, also consider some alternatives if you are contemplating a museum as a lasting way to commemorate a centennial or bicentennial of your community. Is your real goal the preservation of your heritage so that it can become better known, understood in all its aspects, and appreciated by the people of your community? A museum is far from the only way to accomplish that goal.

Many communities observe their major anniversaries by publishing books or commissioning films on their histories, on their natural environments, or on the works of art their areas have inspired. Individual states have sometimes published state histories, state atlases, state encyclopedias, or extensive series of books on aspects of their human and natural history in observance of historical anniversaries. Sometimes historical societies commission commemorative studies from professional writers or trained historians, who are usually affiliated with area colleges. In other instances, historical society members collaborate to produce such books, enlisting knowledgeable amateur historians, local newspaper writers, and volunteers for searches to find photographs.

A popular kind of anniversary project that can engage a community broadly is oral history, resulting in publications or public programs that share with the community what has been learned from interviews with those involved in historical developments, artistic achievements, and nature study. Working under a trained oral historian or at least using authoritative publications on oral history techniques for interviewing people and for evaluating taped testimony, communities can capture the memories of passing generations and can reconstruct significant developments by transcribing and comparing interviews with residents who lived through them. Then the tapes and transcripts can (and should be) made available for ongoing use by depositing them in a historical society, archives, library, or museum.

A good example is a project on the Great Depression that was conducted by the East Tennessee Historical Society in Knoxville. Its staff historians organized volunteers in two counties to interview people who remembered what the depression of the 1930s was like in their region and to search attics and cellars for letters, photographs, and whatever else survived from that trying era. Citizens involved in the project thus learned about their history by doing research themselves. They preserved on tape and in archives much material that otherwise would have been lost about the depression experience. And they summed up their findings in a permanently written record for generations to come.

Other communities have observed anniversaries by identifying historic sites and erecting permanent markers about them, by surveying old buildings in neighborhoods for nomination to the National Register of Historic Places, or by producing newspaper articles, radio broadcasts, films, or television shows on community heritage topics. Also, communities have celebrated themselves more extensively by revitalizing a historic downtown district in collaboration with the Main Street Program of the National Trust for Historic Preservation, by sponsoring the excavation and preservation of archaeological sites, or by establishing county or city archives as permanent repositories for records, photographs, and maps of localities. Special community projects also have included recording information on fading headstones in old cemeteries, rescuing local monuments through the national Save Our Sculpture (SOS) Program, publishing well-researched guide maps to a region's historic features, or commissioning commemorative art works such as sculptures and murals.

One of the potentially most important things that a community can undertake as a special anniversary project is a survey of *all* the kinds of historic resources still surviving and available for study and appreciation. That means checking on the content, condition, and safety of anything that can help the community reconstruct and understand its past, such as local government records, library collections, newspaper files, photographers' portfolios, statues and sculptures on the streets and in parks, television and radio broadcast tapes, historic buildings, sites, neighborhoods, and historic and artistic objects and artifacts that may be moldering away in warehouses as well as accumulating in private collections.

Once historical resources are located, described, and evaluated, then the community can go to work to be sure that the most significant items are permanently saved. Arrangements can be made to secure the most important or valuable documentary materials, rather than simply whatever happens to survive the ravages of time. And the arrangements can be made with existing archives, libraries, historic preservation organizations, and museums without the expense of creating new ones.

For what is important, after all, is not *museums*. What is important is history, art, and nature—the things we are moved by, enjoy, and learn about through the medium of museums. And because no community will ever have enough resources to care completely for everything in its heritage, the wise and prudent course is to identify and spend the available money on saving and providing access to what is most significant.

A collection of political campaign buttons in a local museum is fun to look at, but what meaning does it have if election records have been lost, along with minutes of past political and governmental meetings? What meaning do the political buttons have if there is no surviving photographic or oral history record of the conduct of political campaigns in past periods, of the personalities involved, or of the issues at stake? What do we learn from the buttons if newspaper files reporting political arguments and outcomes have crumbled? And what is our connection to that past if the magnificent old city hall, the architectural pride of the community for fifty or a hundred years and the seat of its most notable political activity, has itself been torn down to make room for a parking lot, instead of adaptively kept in use?

If, after thinking about all this, a museum still seems to you the best way to serve your love of history, of art, of nature, or of the heritage of your community or group, then please proceed in this book to plan the basic steps in getting a museum going. But please do reflect on it. Consider carefully whether you are ready to accept financial, legal, and administrative responsibility for a complex cultural institution, as serious in purpose as a school or library, and to treat its collections in perpetuity with all the manifestations of respect described in these pages. After also considering alternatives described earlier, then ask yourself if you are sure you really want to start a museum.

For More Information

For information on heritage projects and other museum alternatives such as those suggested in this chapter, the following are helpful:

- Bryan, Charles F., Jr., and Mark V. Wetherington, "Hard Times Remembered: A Model Community Project Documents the Depression's Impact on Two East Tennessee Counties," *History News* 39 (August 1984): 28–34

- Dearstyne, Bruce W., *Managing Historical Records Programs: A Guide for Historical Agencies,* AASLH/AltaMira Press, 2000

- George, Gerald W., "Ten Strange Ways to Celebrate a Centennial," *Visiting History, Arguments over Museums and Historic Sites,* AAM, 1990

- Kammen, Carol, *On Doing Local History,* 2nd ed., AASLH/AltaMira Press, 2003

- King, Thomas F., *Places that Count: Traditional Cultural Properties in Cultural Resource Management,* Heritage Resource Management Series/AltaMira Press, 2003

- Kyvig, David E., and Myron A. Marty, *Nearby History: Exploring the Past around You*, 2nd ed., AASLH/AltaMira Press, 2000. AltaMira's AASLH Series also has individual "nearby history" volumes for exploring the history of local schools (by Ronald E. Butchart, 1986), houses and homes (by Barbara Howe et al., 1987), public places (by Gerald Danzer, 1987), places of worship (by James P. Wind, 1990), and local businesses (by K. Austin Kerr et al., 1990)

- National Trust for Historic Preservation, *Threatened Treasures: Creating Lists of Endangered Sites*, National Trust for Historic Preservation, 2001

- Pizer, Laurence R., *A Primer for Local Historical Societies, Revised and Expanded from the First Edition by Dorothy Weyer Creigh*, AASLH/AltaMira Press, 1991 (Includes information on oral history projects, tours, libraries, publishing, site-marking, and historic building preservation)

- Ritchie, Donald A., *Doing Oral History: A Practical Guide*, 2nd ed., Oxford University Press, 2003

- Sommer, Barbara W., and Mary Kay Quinlan, *The Oral History Manual*, AASLH/AltaMira Press, 2002

- Strangstad, Lynette, *A Graveyard Preservation Primer*, AASLH/AltaMira Press, 1993

- Watson, Elizabeth, and Stefan Nagel, *Establishing an Easement Program to Protect Historic, Scenic, and Natural Resources*, National Trust for Historic Preservation, 1980

The following technical leaflets from AASLH also contain information on various kinds of heritage projects:

- *Establishing a Plaque Program* (168)

- *Historical Markers: Planning Local Programs* (104)

- *Historic Walking Tours* (194)

- *Indexing Local Newspapers* (107)
- *Local Historical Records: Programs for Historical Agencies* (121)
- *Preserving the Environment: Participating in the Review Process* (8)

For those interested in attending to historic preservation throughout their communities rather than in one museum, the National Trust for Historic Preservation offers numerous booklets of use in setting up a preservation organization, available individually or as an "Organizational Development Complete Set." Board development, fund-raising, strategic planning, and many other subjects are covered in this series, which is available through www.preservationbooks.org.

For those interested in preserving community statues and sculptures, the following videos from the SOS Project of the Smithsonian Institution's Museum of American Art and the National Institute for the Conservation of Cultural Property are available through the Heritage Preservation organization and AASLH:

- *Legacy at Risk: Strategies to Save Outdoor Sculpture* (1994)
- *A Video Guide for the SOS Volunteer* (1992)

Concerning local records and persuading your government officials to give them better care, AASLH offers a series of twelve technical leaflets, developed at AASLH by the National Information Center for Local Government Records. AASLH also rents an audiovisual program about local government records care entitled *Guardians of the Public Record.*

Concerning war memorabilia, for which many veterans or their families seem to be seeking museum homes, good alternatives to new museums are the ones already established by the U.S. armed forces, which can be identified by contacting the following military authorities:

- U.S. Air Force
  Curator, U.S. Air Force Museum
  1100 Spaatz Street
  Wright-Patterson AFB, OH 45433-7102
  (937) 255-7204, ext. 337
  usaf.museum@wpafb.af.mil

- U.S. Army
  Staff Curator, U.S. Army Center of Military History, Attn:
      DAMH-MD
  103 3rd Avenue
  Fort McNair, DC 20319-5058
  (202) 685-2451
  terry.vanmeter@hqda.army.mil

- U.S. Coast Guard
  Historian's Office
  2100 2nd Street, SW
  Washington, DC 20593
  (202) 267-2596
  rbrowning@comdt.uscg.mil

- U.S. Marine Corps
  Curator, Marine Corps Museum
  2014 Anderson Avenue
  Quantico, VA 22134-5002
  (703) 784-2606
  christmask@nt.quantico.usmc.mil

- U.S. Navy
  Director, Naval Historical Center
  805 Kidder Breese Street, SE
  Washington Navy Yard, DC 20374-5060
  (202) 433-2318
  mark.wertheimer@navy.mil

Museum of South Texas History. In a new wing of the Museum of South Texas History, in Edinburg, Texas, this cast of the skeleton of a mammoth brings the region's prehistory to life for two students. Photo courtesy of the Museum of South Texas History.

5

And If You Are Planning a Historic House Museum?

Think about it: Within a Sunday afternoon's drive from where you live, how many historic building museums are there already? If your community is like most, the answer would be at least a half-dozen. If you live in a fairly populous place, the answer could be a dozen or more. If you live in a major metropolitan area, thirty to fifty would not be exceptional. Can you—do you want to—compete with all those others for money, visitors, staff, and volunteers?

Think about it: How many of the historic building museums you can drive to in a Sunday afternoon are alike? If you live in the South, how many of them are antebellum plantation houses? If you live in the Northeast, how many are homes from the eighteenth century? In the Midwest, Victorian mansions? In the Southwest, Spanish adobes? And everywhere, mills, log cabins, train stations, and one-room schools? Will your museum interpret a building of a kind that is already interpreted in your area? Can you explain how yours will be so different as to draw visitors who already have seen the others?

Think about it: How many of the historic building museums within that Sunday afternoon's drive give visitors the same thing? "Welcome, a tour will be available in half an hour." "This is the parlor where the family entertained visitors." "Please stay behind the cordon and don't touch the things you see." What will you do differently for visitors? Will it be different enough to attract enough of them?

Think about it: How many historic building museums in your region show or say the same things every time you visit? In fact, how many do you visit repeatedly? How many have you even visited twice? It is tough to attract repeat visitors when what you are exhibiting mainly is an unchanging building with an unchanging set of furnishings. Can you vary your program enough throughout the year that people will keep returning?

Think about it: How many historic building museums within driving distance of your location are open half-days, on weekends only, or just by appointment? How many seem scruffy or are suffering from deferred maintenance to the point that even you can see where the roof is leaking and the plaster is peeling? How many cannot afford to pay staff? How many always seem in financial trouble? How many are consuming funds that might help historic preservation more if spent by groups on advocacy, adaptive use strategies, historic property surveys, historic district demarcations, National Register nominations, private-owner assistance, and other activities that help save more than just one building?

Think about it: How many historic building museums that you can reach in a Sunday afternoon are not reaching the communities around them? How many operate as elite institutions in the midst of decayed neighborhoods? How many ignore the interests of all groups but the one that runs them? How many of these groups are simply "playing house"? How will you connect with diverse audiences? How will you persuade all kinds of people that the stories your building can tell will relate to them if they will chance a visit?

If you have good, positive answers to all these questions, then please go ahead full tilt and make use of the rest of this book. Your capacities will match your enthusiasm. But such questions have arisen nationwide as the number of historic house museums has mushroomed. The last half-century has seen many wonderful building museums develop; it has also seen many fall into a kind of limbo in which they neither really prosper nor fully die.

Preservationists have abandoned the notion that to save an old building one *must* make it into a museum. Preservationists condone the careful—and caring—use of historic structures for commercial purposes, for nonmuseum community facilities, for offices, and even for private residences. The National Trust for Historic Preservation, its closest regional office, your state historic preservation office, or a local preservation organization that will almost surely be somewhere within the range of your Sunday drive can help you identify workable alternatives.

Think about it.

For More Information

Two articles summing up the situation confronting historic building museums appeared in *Forum Journal, the Journal of the National Trust for Historic Preservation* in its spring 2002 (vol. 16, no. 3) issue:

- George, Gerald, "Historic House Museum Malaise: A Conference Considers What's Wrong." 12–19
- Moe, Richard, "Are There Too Many House Museums?" 4–11

Options for alternative uses of historic buildings are identified in:

- Berkowitz, Nina, ed., *New Life for White Elephants: Adapting Historic Buildings for New Uses*, National Trust for Historic Preservation, 1996 (the National Trust also has individual books on the rehabilitation and adaptive use of schools, theaters, and farm buildings)

PART II

HOW BEST TO GO ABOUT IT

Mary McLeod Bethune Council House National Historic Site of the National Park Service. This row house in Washington, D.C., now a house museum of the National Park Service, was historically the headquarters of the National Council of Negro Women. Photo courtesy of the National Park Service, Mary McLeod Bethune Council House archives.

6

Analyze for Essentials

If you have now thought it through and concluded, yes, a museum is feasible for you, the time has come to work out an outline for planning it. This plan will be started by preparing to answer twenty important questions, four of which will be covered in each of the next five chapters. The following are all of the questions so that you can see where you are headed:

1. What is your museum's mission and its limits?

2. What collections are available or need to be found to serve your museum's purpose?

3. What physical facilities will work for your museum?

4. What provisions will you need for security?

5. Who will have responsibility for your museum?

6. What rules will govern its operations?

7. What divisions of labor and allocations of authority will there be?

8. How will harmonious working relationships be maintained?

9. What will be your collections policy?

10. What conservation needs must you meet and how?

11. What provisions will you make for ongoing research?

12. What interpretive methods will you use to reach your publics?

13. What time schedule for development will the museum follow?

14. Who will direct your museum and how will you recruit that person?

15. What staff positions, paid and volunteer, will be needed?

16. What provisions will you make for staff training in museum work and museum ethics?

17. How will you cope with change?

18. How will you conduct ongoing planning?

19. How will you evaluate your museum's activities?

20. How will you keep your museum alive, dynamic, creative, even visionary, and closely connected to your community?

This is your checklist for planning. This little book cannot hand you answers to these twenty questions for your specific museum. The following pages can help you understand what is required overall for museum development so you can develop your plan's answers with confidence that you will not be overlooking essential needs or major concerns.

That said, let us begin with *this* chapter's museum-planning checklist questions—the first four on the previous list—covering your museum's mission, its collections and facilities for carrying out that mission, and security for collections, facilities, staff, and visitors.

Let's take up the first question: What sort of museum will yours be? You will need to assess the museum materials (buildings and collections) you possess and the subjects they cover. Some possibilities follow in the form of what museum people (and other strategic planners) call *mission statements.* The following is a range of examples from real museums:

- "The Johnson County Museums [*sic*] is committed to expanding the public's sense of community through an understanding of the county's history and its place in American society. To achieve this purpose, the Museums collects and preserves artifacts and information that document the county's heritage, and produces interpretive exhibits, educational programs, and publications. The Museums is dedicated to the belief that we can learn from the past to understand better the present and future." (Johnson County Museums, Shawnee, Kansas)

- "The Mission of the Arizona-Sonora Desert Museum is to inspire people to live in harmony with the natural world by fostering love, appreciation, and understanding of the Sonoran Desert." (Arizona-Sonora Desert Museum, Tucson, Arizona)

- "We are a non-profit institution dedicated to interpreting and preserving the [art]work and life of Charles M. Russell, as well as that of his contemporaries." (C. M. Russell Museum, Great Falls, Montana)

- "The Mission of Drayton Hall, a historic site of the National Trust for Historic Preservation, is to preserve and interpret Drayton Hall and its environs in order to educate the public and inspire people to embrace historic preservation." (Drayton Hall, Charleston, South Carolina)

- "The Mission of the Center is to educate the public about African American history and culture from the African origins to the present by collecting, preserving, and interpreting material evidence of the Black experience." (National Afro-American Museum and Cultural Center, Dayton, Ohio)

- "We collect, preserve, interpret, and exhibit works of art and present related educational programs in support of the teaching, research, and public service mission of the

University of Wisconsin, Madison. We do this because the visual arts enrich individual human experience and because knowledge of art is essential to understanding diverse cultures, past and present." (Elvehjem Museum of Art, University of Wisconsin, Madison)

- "History San José involves diverse audiences in exploring the varieties of human experience that contribute to the continuing history of San José and the Santa Clara Valley." (History San José, California)

- "The Pratt Museum is dedicated to the process of Education, exploring the natural environment and human experience relative to the Kachemak Bay region of Alaska and its place in the world. The Museum seeks to inspire self-reflection and dialogue in its community and visitors through exhibitions, programs, and collections in the arts, sciences, and humanities." (The Pratt Museum, Homer, Alaska)

- "The Southern Alleghenies Museum of Art exists to preserve, exhibit, and advance American art and is dedicated to making its programs and activities accessible to the people of the southwestern area of central Pennsylvania. Charged with the development, maintenance, and perpetuation of a permanent collection, the Museum mounts exhibitions designed to evoke an interest in and an understanding and appreciation of American art." (Southern Alleghenies Museum of Art, Loretto, Pennsylvania)

- "The Lower East Side Tenement Museum's mission is: to promote tolerance and historical perspective through the presentation and interpretation of the variety of immigrant and migrant experiences on Manhattan's Lower East Side, a gateway to America." (Lower East Side Tenement Museum, National Trust for Historic Preservation, New York City)

- "The Alexander & Baldwin Sugar Museum is a non-profit organization dedicated to preserving and presenting the history and heritage of the sugar industry and the multiethnic plantation life which it engendered." (Alexander & Baldwin Sugar Museum, Puunene, Maui, Hawaii)

All of these examples show that no one statement of mission or purpose suits every museum. You will need to analyze what you want your museum to accomplish and describe that clearly and concretely in a mission statement of your own.

As you do that, be sure to analyze the *limits* of your intent. The most useful and meaningful museum self-definitions are those that clarify boundaries that museums will observe. The boundaries may be on the kinds of objects collected, the period of history covered, the developments to be documented, the area to be served, the group or area whose heritage is to be preserved, or some other defining focus.

Identifying the limits of your intent is necessary to save you from accumulating a haphazard hodgepodge of stuff that will confuse your public, overflow your facilities, consume your re-sources, and ultimately put your museum at cross-purposes. So, early in your planning, determine what limits you will place on your museum's coverage and establish it in a formal mission statement of scope and purpose.

That statement will become your basic guide to everything else. For example, if you plan a nature center type of museum with live specimens, the old post office you have been offered downtown is not likely to be a useful museum facility. If you in-tend to document and illustrate the history of your region or group, then you are not going to use up your acquisitions budget on an international ceramics collection however won-derful the ceramics may be. And if your purpose is to preserve and exhibit a splendid international collection of ceramics, clearly you will not be in the market for stuffed, two-headed calves or Conestoga wagons, but the old post office downtown might suit your ceramic museum's needs beautifully.

Thus, once you have defined your mission, it will help you evaluate and provide for two other essentials that need analysis from the beginning: collections and facilities. Whether or not you possess one or the other at the outset, your plan must spell out what you will do about both.

Chapter 8 will discuss your need for a formal collections pol-icy. The question now is whether the collections, if any, with which you are starting the museum will adequately serve its mission, as you have defined it, or whether a substantial search for suitable objects will be necessary even before you consider opening your doors.

Perhaps you will want to avoid the expense and trouble of developing and caring for collections of your own. In that event, your plan must identify sources of traveling exhibits that will serve the purpose of your museum and be available to it. A few museums do not maintain extensive collections of their own but organize special exhibits through arrangements to borrow temporarily from the collections of others. This approach has its own problems, however, such as the need to be able to ensure donating museums that you can be trusted to provide security, insurance, and competence in using their works of art or artifacts safely and meaningfully. Museums that lend objects will have, and can explain to you, standards that a recipient museum must meet.

In considering the borrowing option, analyze what is available from your state's museum or historical society, from other individual museums, from the American Federation of Arts (which offers exhibits to members), and from the Smithsonian Institution Traveling Exhibition Service. The Smithsonian also has a Smithsonian Affiliations program through which it shares artifacts, programs, and expertise with other museums. (In 2003, the Smithsonian had 129 museum partners in 37 states.) The availability of traveling exhibits is often announced in the newsletters of the American Association for State and Local History (AASLH), the American Association of Museums (AAM), and other museum service organizations. Regional, state, and provincial (in Canada) associations of museums may also be able to help you identify available traveling exhibits.

Most likely, however, you will need to acquire collections suitable for carrying out your particular mission or to fill gaps in such collections as you already possess. For example, if your museum collects regional art, is some artist of consequence who worked in your region underrepresented in the collection you have been given? If your museum's purpose is to show the relationships of the peculiarities of your region's climate and environment to the kinds of plant and animal life that exist there, do you have enough specimens or pictorial material on birds, fish, mammals, and reptiles to do that? For your history museum, what kinds of surviving objects were significant in each phase of your region's development or representative of life in each period? What is still available to document its diverse peoples, transportation developments, farming, mining, business, industry, labor, churches, schools, cultural institutions, ethnic communities, wearing apparel, pastimes, government, politics, social relations, community achievements, losses, and hardships? How much additional collecting will you need to create a representative collection that can effectively document multiple stories? To judge what is needed to make a collection representative, you may need help from subject matter experts, who might be found on the faculties of colleges and universities near you.

In short, planning for collections means assessing, on the basis of your mission, the collections already available to you, how much and what kinds of additional material you need to seek, who will do it, where, and over what period of time. Specificity is desirable to identify the material you hope to add within the next three to five years and the ways in which you will go about it.

If adequate collections are possible, what then about adequate facilities?

Whether you hope to build a new structure for your museum or adapt an old one, planning for it begins with a list of each kind of activity you may need to carry on within it. Many museums find that they need space for offices, meetings, exhibits, and storage of collections, supplies, and maintenance materials. Also, museums often need shops for exhibit fabrication and for cleaning and conserving objects, a kitchen for catering receptions, a research library and archives, space for training volunteers, an audiovisual theater, events space, and a gift shop. Which of those and what other kinds of space will the particularities of your museum require?

Above all, avoid the initial mistake of supposing that space for exhibits is the primary consideration. In most museums, storage and work areas equal or exceed exhibit space. The general rule for allocation of space in museum structures has been to allot 40 percent for exhibits, 40 percent for storage, and 20 percent for offices and other activities.

Keeping those percentages in mind, analyze the *utility* of the space in any building you may be offered. A superb Victorian mansion, for example, may have small rooms that pose serious problems for substantial exhibits, visitor traffic flow, and collection security. High ceilings and lots of windows may make it difficult or expensive to maintain the proper ranges of temperature and relative humidity or the protection from direct sunlight that museum collections, both on exhibit and in storage, need to inhibit deterioration. Structural changes needed to solve such problems may run afoul of historic preservation standards for maintaining old buildings—a historic structure is itself a valuable artifact that will suffer if not maintained with respect for the integrity of its historical and architectural character. For example, if making space for an exhibit about President Abraham Lincoln in the preserved Ford Theater building in Washington, D.C., required tearing out the theater box where he was sitting when fatally shot, history would clearly be ill served.

If at all possible, enlist an architect, an experienced museum professional, and a knowledgeable historic preservationist to help you analyze an existing building for problems that may cause you grief and cost you money if you do not recognize them before starting a museum operation. Does the roof need replacing? Is the building constructed so that you can expect to use it for a museum for at least fifty to one hundred years? Does it have insulation that will hold down utility bills? Can the wall surfaces be easily cleaned and used for exhibition purposes? What about the paint? Surfaces need to be attractive but also easy to clean and maintain. Will the floor covering survive several thousand visitors a year, especially if they track in mud and moisture from rain and snow? Can you make the building comply with legal requirements for access for the elderly and disabled? Can the climate be controlled with affordable air conditioning and heating units? Does the electrical wiring meet commercial standards and government codes? Are there enough circuits for lighting exhibits, galleries, offices, and program areas as well as for outside lights, security systems, evening receptions and programs, and shop equipment without risking blown fuses and fires? Is the plumbing adequate for public restrooms and water fountains, as well as for the kitchen? Is there room outside for adequate parking?

Please avoid the assumption, however, that a history museum has to be in an old building. Unused space available in a relatively new building may be just as acceptable for a history museum as it is for other purposes. Whatever kind of museum you plan, a new building might more readily be made to suit your needs—but again, only if you analyze the needs carefully and honestly. Ideally, you will choose an architect who has museum design experience. Since such specialists are rare, look for an architect who is at least willing to study the special requirements of museum design in consultation with museum professionals.

What construction material will go into your new or rehabilitated museum? Wood siding, composition shingles, and wood decking are neither cheap to buy nor easy to maintain. Masonry construction lasts longer; how long will you intend the structure to serve your museum? Will the architecture of the building itself express the museum's nature and purpose? Will it relate in desirable ways to the architecture of nearby buildings and the character of the neighborhood around it? Will the site allow for possible future expansion along with adequate access, traffic control, and parking? Is it sufficiently close to public transportation? Will the design enable visitors to be easily monitored in the exhibit areas but also allow quick exit in case of fire or other natural disaster? These are important questions to ask your architect. Finding an appropriate architect can be facilitated by contacting a local chapter of the American Institute of Architects or its national office at 1735 New York Avenue, NW, Washington, DC 20006; (800) 242-3837; www.aia.org.

Since the terrorist attack of September 11, 2001, on the World Trade Center and the Pentagon, the entire nation has become more security conscious, museums included. Some large, national museums have instituted new precautions such as adding guards and checking visitors' bags. The chance that an international terrorist will select a community museum outside a major metropolitan area for a target seems remote, but there are other kinds of terrorists. These include the destructive attention-seekers, deranged iconoclasts, and common vandals, burglars, and arsonists who threaten all museums.

Insurance is an insufficient solution; most museum objects are irreplaceable. From the beginning it is wise to plan how you will secure your staff, visitors, collections, and buildings against thieves and assailants as well as against fire and natural forces. The need for many common security devices, such as fire extinguishers and dead bolts on doors, will be obvious to you. But additionally, even the smallest museum can improve its security by the way it lights its building, landscapes its grounds, and manages its visitors. These are considerations to bring up with an architect, to discuss with local law enforcement authorities, and to ask other museums about. A security checklist for small museums is listed among the sources of more information at the end of this chapter.

One final caution. It is easy to think of your building as the museum itself and invest the bulk of your resources in just the housing for collections and activities. Be sure that your budgeting takes into consideration *all* essential expenditures.

So, now you know what essentials you must analyze as the first part of your plan. You are ready to start answering these questions in the museum-planning checklist:

1. What is your museum's mission and its limits?

2. What collections are available or need to be found to serve your museum's purpose?

3. What physical facilities will work for your museum?

4. What provisions will you need for security?

For More Information

Concerning mission statements, the following is useful:

- Anderson, Gail, ed., *Museum Mission Statements: Building a Distinct Identity*, AAM, 1998

Concerning museum physical facilities, the following are useful:

- American Institute of Architects, *You and Your Architect*, www.aia.org/consumer/youandyourarchitect.pdf

- Rosenblatt, Arthur, *Building Type Basics for Museum Facilities*, John Wiley and Sons, 2001

Concerning museum security, the following are useful:

- Liston, David, ed., *Museum Security and Protection: A Handbook for Cultural Heritage Institutions*, International Committee on Museum Security, ICOM, and Routledge, 1993

- Leo, Jack, *Basic Security Checklist for the Small Museum*, available on request by phone at (281) 337-9292, by e-mail at longjack@wt.net, or by mail at 5100 Ecret, Dickinson, TX 77539

The following technical leaflets published by AASLH also are pertinent to several subjects covered in this chapter:

- *Before Restoration Begins: Keeping Your Historic House Intact* (62)

- *Collecting Historical Artifacts: An Aid for Small Museums* (6)

- *How to Write a Furnishing Plan* (218)

- *Protecting Cultural Heritage Properties from Fire* (206)

History San José. History San José in California, which interprets multiple historic sites and collections, involves visitors in museum programs such as this archaeological activity. Photo courtesy of History San José, San José, California.

7

Organize for Operation

Now that you have specified your museum's mission and made plans for its collections, facilities, and security, you are ready to plan its operating organization. You can begin to answer the museum-planning checklist questions about rules and responsibilities, divisions of labor, lines of authority, and harmonious working relations. You know enough of what the museum will be and do to draft its constitution and bylaws.

These may not necessarily be the terms you will use. Constitutions with bylaws are usually the governing documents of museums that are organized, operated, and primarily supported by groups of private citizens. Such museums should incorporate under their state's laws as nonprofit, tax-exempt corporations, in which case the articles of incorporation become a basic governing document. If the museum belongs to a county or municipality, its governing document may be the ordinance by which the county or city council establishes it. If some other governing body, such as a college or university, creates the museum, its governing document may be a charter that grants specified rights and powers from and within the larger organization.

All such documents, however, essentially serve the same purposes and cover the same matters. They define the museum, authorize its operation, and describe the ways in which power will be organized, exercised, and limited within the institution. Such a governing document must be established in accordance with federal, state, and local laws and must be adopted formally by whatever duly constituted body will have authority over the museum: a city or county council, a university board of regents, a group of incorporators, or whoever else may take legal responsibility for the museum. Once adopted, the governing document should be treated as having the force of law in the museum's operations.

If you cannot get legal assistance donated, you will need to retain an attorney to draft your governing document. Knowledge of the law in your state and locality will help particularly with the parts of the document that establish the legal existence of the museum organization, authorize its perpetual operation, describe the limits of liability of its trustees or members, specify its tax status, declare its right to hold property and receive gifts, and provide for what will happen to its assets if it should cease operation.

Also, you would do well to apply for tax-exempt status from the U.S. Internal Revenue Service (IRS) under the federal internal revenue code (or in Canada from the Department of Internal Revenue), particularly if your museum wants to attract donations of collections and cash. Designation by the IRS as a tax-exempt educational or charitable organization not only saves your museum from having to pay federal taxes, but also allows donors to your museum to reduce their income tax liability by the portion of the monetary value of their gifts that can be subtracted from their taxable income. This is a powerful incentive for businesses and individuals to make gifts. They can contribute to the cultural enrichment of their communities while also reducing what they otherwise would owe in taxes. However, they cannot take "charitable deductions" for gifts to a museum unless that museum has met standards for tax exemption and has been granted tax-exempt status by the IRS. The internal revenue code specifies that museums, themselves, can avoid paying most taxes and can assure donors of tax write-offs for their gifts only if they are "organized and operated exclusively for one or more of the purposes enumerated as allowed by the federal regulations governing tax-exempt organizations." Therefore, your constitution, charter, articles of incorporation, or enabling ordinance should specify that your museum is serving one or more of those purposes. For lists of approved purposes, forms, and other information about applying for tax-exempt status, contact your area's IRS office, check your telephone book for a toll-free IRS number, or consult the IRS website (www.irs.gov). What else should be in a museum's basic governing document? Typically, it contains articles or paragraphs answering these questions:

- What is the name of the corporation or organization and its general nature (including nonprofit status)?

- What are its purposes?

- Where is it incorporated or chartered and what is its official location?

- How is it governed, including how it designates officers and trustees?

- What specific powers will it have, such as the power to receive gifts, hold property, enter into contracts, appoint agents and employees, and carry out activities?

- By what procedure can its governing documents be amended?

Depending on state legal requirements, a governing document may also include the authorization of a public notary, the intended duration of the organization, the names and addresses of its incorporators or organizers and any registered agents they may have, provisions for membership, and a dissolution clause providing for the disposition of assets in the event that the museum should shut down. Also, your museum may want to specify that it will provide itself with liability insurance.

In addition to the primary governing document, most museums also have bylaws, which provide procedural detail, particularly about things that are likely to need changing from time to time. Bylaws typically spell out the roles and responsibilities of governing boards and of individuals who will carry out board policies, such as an executive director. A museum's bylaws typically follow this outline:

1. Name of the museum and governing organization
2. Purpose(s)
3. Board of directors (trustees, or equivalent policy-setting body)
   a. Number, qualifications, and terms of office
   b. Procedures for nominations and elections
   c. Procedures for removal
   d. Procedures for filling vacancies
   e. Place, time, and requirements for announcing official meetings
   f. Quorum requirements
   g. Committees of the board
4. Officers
   a. Number and method of election or selection
   b. Powers and duties
   c. Removal procedures
5. Members (if any) of the museum
   a. Membership classifications
   b. Dues and benefits
   c. Meetings, provisions for providing notice, and any quorum requirement
6. Advisory bodies (if any)
   a. Appointment requirements and procedures
   b. Powers and duties
7. Financial provisions
   a. Definition of the museum's fiscal year
   b. Who has authority to sign checks and transfer funds
   c. Who has authority to enter into contracts
   d. Who has authority to accept gifts and donations
   e. Budget preparation and financial reporting requirements
8. Amendment procedures

A sample set of museum bylaws is in document C.

Please note that constitutions and bylaws are not mere legal formalities or window dressing. You will suffer if you put anything into your governing documents that you do not intend to live by. Also, it helps to draft such documents as clearly and precisely as you can, so that those who will be legally responsible under them clearly understand the requirements from the outset.

In the bylaws, or in additions to them, take special care to make clear the differences between the responsibilities of board members or trustees and the responsibilities of the executive director and staff, whether paid or volunteer. More conflict arises in museums from failures to understand and respect the division between the role of trustees and the role of the staff director than from any other cause. The standard distinction is that the board sets policy, which the staff carries out. For example, the board approves a proposal from the staff director to create a new exhibit, and the board authorizes expenditures for it as part of an annual budget that the board has approved. Staff should respect the right of the board to say yes or no to a major expenditure for such a purpose. But if the board does authorize the exhibit, then board members should let the staff create it, using the professional judgment and experience for which the board hired the staff. A staff director or curator who goes ahead with a major exhibit that the board rejected or did not provide for within the approved budget is exceeding his or her authority. On the other hand, a board member who walks into the museum and proceeds to tell staff which artifacts to use in an approved exhibit, how to design it, what to write in the exhibit labels, and which firm to hire to print the labels is overstepping the bounds of a trustee's role. Also, to be effective in day-to-day operations of the museum, the staff director needs a free hand to hire and fire personnel, paid and volunteer. That should not be a prerogative of the board, but it is entitled to hold the director responsible for any good or harm that the staff may do.

The staff director should be held accountable for expenditures authorized in the budget and responsible for the quality of the museum within budgetary strictures. But the director cannot produce quality work within budgetary limitations without the freedom to make disbursements, choose vendors, and exercise judgment about how to achieve quality in an authorized activity.

If the board gives the director full authority to carry out approved activities and then is not happy with the quality of the results, the board has the right to replace the director.

This is true whether the director is paid or volunteering. It is easy on the budget to let some talented citizen or even an unpaid member of the board provide day-to-day administrative direction. But such volunteers can thumb their noses at boards more easily than can paid staff members, who value both their salaries and their professional reputations. All too often, an individual with great energy and enthusiasm volunteers to run a museum for a board that is relieved to turn it over to someone—anyone—with the result that the museum eventually gets the image of belonging to that dedicated individual, who begins to confuse him- or herself with the board and insists on deciding unilaterally what to do as well as how to do it. As more people feel ignored and excluded, such a "mom and pop" museum eventually loses public interest and support.

On the other hand, particularly when the staff director is able and energetic, trustees often begin to expect her or him to do even the things for which trustees have particular responsibility. It will not hurt to reiterate that helping to organize a lobbying effort or a fund-raising campaign may be an appropriate staff activity, but the trustees are ultimately responsible for securing the necessary funds. They are the people with influence who can ask others for money. The old cliché is that members of a museum board should follow the "three Gs": "give, get, or get off." No board will be able to keep competent staff long if, every year, the director and staff must go out by themselves and, in effect, raise their own salaries.

In museums so small that no professional staff has yet been hired—or museums that have, at most, a paid director—boards sometimes designate committees to help carry out such activities as publicity, acquisitions for the collections, or even exhibit preparations and special programs, as well as fund-raising. Even in these instances, however, final authority for decisions about ways to carry out an approved project should be vested in an individual who is designated as the administrator of the museum, paid or unpaid.

A wise director will know how to exercise such authority without seeming dictatorial to committee chairs and members. And a wise director will keep the board well informed about the progress of all activities, as well as alerted to anything that is not going well or is potentially controversial or dangerous. A wise board, and particularly its president or chairperson and executive committee, will regularly review the quality of the museum's activities and will let the director know of any concern about his or her performance at the earliest convenient moment after that concern arises. More than one board president has felt unduly excluded from the museum's activities by a director who has preferred to operate in the dark. And more than one director has been dismissed before receiving any inkling that the board was upset about anything. Candid, open communication, even when opinions are in conflict, can be the road to ultimate harmony.

The best way to keep expectations clear is to set evaluation standards in writing along with work and performance plans. The board can negotiate such standards and plans with the director, and the director with others on the staff. There is room for give and take in parceling out roles and responsibilities. But it is imperative that officers, board members, paid staff, and volunteers all clearly understand and accept the rules, whatever they are, about who has authority to do what, and who will be held responsible for the results. The board itself should see that the rules are followed by its own members, as well as by the director, who must take responsibility for the staff's compliance.

Planning an operating organization goes beyond written actions such as codifying the rules in a constitution and bylaws, charter, or ordinance. Some museums find it useful to have special meetings, particularly once a museum is operational, for the purpose of going over the governing documents, raising and resolving questions of authority and responsibility, and orienting new board members or new staff directors to the expectations of the organization. There is nothing like a cordial reception, perhaps even a cocktail party, to provide a warm, friendly, human setting for introducing a newcomer to the board or staff and outlining the ground rules.

On that cheerful note, and with a look at the first two documents in the back of this book—Document A: Basic Organization Chart and Document B: Board Membership Responsibilities Agreement—the organizational part of your planning can begin, and you may start answering the next four questions in the museum-planning checklist, which deal with operating the museum:

5. Who will have responsibility for your museum?
6. What rules will govern its operations?
7. What divisions of labor and allocations of authority will there be?
8. How will harmonious working relationships be maintained?

For More Information

The following may be useful on museum governance in general:

- Adams, Roxana, ed., *Foundations of Museum Governance for Private Nonprofit Museums*, a Technical Information Service Resource Pack, American Association of Museums (AAM), 2002

- Adams, Roxana, ed., *Foundations of Governance for Museums in Non-museum Parent Organizations*, a Technical Information Service Resource Pack, AAM, 2002

- Genoways, Hugh H., and Lynne M. Ireland, *Museum Administration: An Introduction*, AASLH/AltaMira Press, 2003

- Malaro, Marie C., *Museum Governance: Mission, Ethics, Policy*, Smithsonian Institution Press, 1994

The following may be useful on governance documents:

- Fletcher, Kathleen, *The Policy Sampler: A Resource for Nonprofit Boards*, BoardSource, 2000

- Perry, Kenneth D., ed., *The Museum Forms Book*, 3rd ed., Texas Association of Museums, 1999

The following may be useful concerning boards of trustees and advisory committees:

- Andringa, Robert C., and Ted W. Engstrom, *Nonprofit Board Answer Book: Practical Guidelines for Board Members and Chief Executives*, BoardSource, 2002

- Axelrod, Nancy R., *The Advisory Committee*, BoardSource, 1998

- Chait, Richard P., *How to Help Your Board Govern More and Manage Less*, rev. ed., BoardSource, 2003

- Houchin, Susan, and Candace Widmer, *The Art of Trusteeship: The Nonprofit Board Member's Guide to Effective Governance*, Jossey-Bass, 2000

- Howe, Fisher, *Welcome to the Board*, Jossey-Bass, 1995

- Hughes, Sandra R., et al., *The Board Building Cycle: Nine Steps to Finding, Recruiting, and Engaging Nonprofit Board Members*, BoardSource, 2000

- Ingram, Richard T., *Ten Basic Responsibilities of Nonprofit Boards*, BoardSource, 2003

- Kurtz, Daniel, *Managing Conflicts of Interest: Practical Guidelines for Nonprofit Boards*, BoardSource, 2001

- Light, Mark, *The Strategic Board: The Step-by-Step Guide to High-Impact Governance*, John Wiley and Sons, 2001

- Naumer, Helmuth J., *Of Mutual Respect and Other Things: Thoughts on Museum Trusteeship*, AAM, 1989

- Skramstad, Harold, and Susan Skramstad, *A Handbook for Museum Trustees*, AAM and the Museum Trustee Association, 2003

The C. M. Russell Log Studio in Great Falls, Montana. The studio is part of the C. M. Russell Museum, which exhibits the work of Russell and other Western artists. Photo courtesy of the C. M. Russell Museum.

8

Plan for Activities

By now you may be thinking, "I have gone through all the complicated conceptual and organizational tasks. I have specified a
mission for my museum. I have located collections and facilities.
I have arranged for security. I have set up an organization, ready
to go operational, with all the legal bases covered. All the rules,
roles, and responsibilities are clear. I have done all that. Now can
I plan the fun things—programs, exhibit openings, receptions,
champagne!?"

Not quite yet. Your museum still is not ready to plan festive
ribbon-cuttings or grand unveilings. First come provisions for
the continuing background functions that are essential for everything a museum presents to its public. Several ongoing activities
are what now need to be added to your plan. So this chapter will
deal with the museum-planning checklist questions about collection work, conservation, research, and interpretation.

First: collecting. Your plan for this is going to require another
document: a written collections policy. This policy is almost as
important as your museum's constitution or other basic governing document. The collections policy is also a tool for sticking
with your mission statement against a lot of otherwise confusing
pressures.

For example, suppose your museum's formally established
mission is to preserve physical evidence of the history of your
city. But one day, your Uncle Joe comes in with a big-hearted

look to announce that, in church last Sunday, he realized he should give the museum all the mounted wild-animal heads he has been accumulating from years of summertime safaris. What do you say? You realize that the heads are more relevant to Kenya than to your city's history, that they would take up more room than anything already in your collection, and that the expense of repairing the moth-eaten ones would drain staff time and money. But how can you refuse generous Uncle Joe?

Or, what do you do when one of your museum's trustees wants to give you a collection of artworks by a nineteenth-century artist who painted scenes in your region? That is, the trustee will give you the collection if you give the museum's support to an inflated appraisal of the paintings' monetary value so that the trustee can take a substantial tax write-off.

Or, what do you do if, ten years after a businessman has given his exquisite, locally made furniture to your museum, his heirs decide they want the collection back and insist that it was only on loan?

And what do you do if you find the president of your museum's board either borrowing a piece of that fine furniture for use at home or throwing some of it away because he or she thinks it is space consuming and ugly?

In all these instances, you can say this: "No, I'm really sorry, I'd like to accommodate you, but I can't go against the museum's formally adopted collection policy." However, you can do that only when you have a written, board-endorsed collection policy.

Often, when a group begins to operate a museum, one of the great temptations is to accept any old or interesting object just because it is nice and will help to fill exhibit space. But a museum is not a community attic, and most particularly it is not a dumping ground for white elephants—things that people no longer want but cannot bear to throw away. So the collections policy starts with your mission statement and then spells out the kinds of things that the museum wants and does not want. Also, it outlines procedures that must be followed for deciding whether to accept a gift or approve a purchase. It specifies procedure that must be followed for discarding things from the collection or letting them for any reason leave the museum permanently. Sometimes, museums specify that the director, a special acquisition or collection committee, or the entire governing board of the museum must formally approve before any object may be accepted, purchased, sold, traded, lent, thrown out, given away, or taken away. This helps to prevent arbitrary action by any individual staff member or trustee, along with theft, negligence, bad judgment, and actions taken in response to pressure. It also helps to prevent hurt feelings, upset supporters, and even lawsuits.

Trouble with the U.S. Internal Revenue Service can be avoided if the collections policy forbids anyone connected with the museum to appraise the value of gifts for tax purposes. There is nothing wrong with encouraging donors to recognize the legitimate tax benefits to which they may be entitled if they give valuable objects, but for financial appraisals they should be referred to independent experts not connected with the museum. Collections policies also can reduce conflict-of-interest problems by forbidding staff members to collect personally, or traffic in, the kinds of objects that the museum collects.

As a general rule, good collections policies forbid accepting objects if donors place conditions on their use or ultimate disposition. Fewer disputes occur when material that comes with unalterable conditions is accepted on loan only for a brief, specified period of time, for study, or for use in some temporary exhibit. Otherwise, the museum is well advised to seek full title to anything it accepts or purchases, including the right to dispose of the item by sale, trade, or any other means, at the museum's discretion following procedures in its collections policy. Donors may prefer to make unrestricted gifts of valuable material if they know the museum has a formal collections policy that will prevent arbitrary treatment of donated material by unauthorized individuals.

Additionally, a museum should avoid gifts that come with restrictions on the museum's ability to exhibit effectively. Gifts can cause a museum future headaches if donors insist that all items in a collection be forever displayed together, that a donated artifact always be kept on permanent exhibit, or that the donor's name be perpetually displayed in a prominent way with such an exhibit. So the collections policy should also identify unacceptable restrictions on gifts.

Finally, the collections policy should specify what is to be done once an item is accepted. When an object arrives, formal record-keeping about it needs to begin. A *standard object cataloging record* (see document G), sometimes called an *accession sheet,* will identify the source and nature of each new object or collection. Following the accessioning of items, condition evaluations and documentary research should proceed as soon as possible and also be recorded.

As observed earlier, *registration* is what museum people call this kind of record keeping. Without it, things will be as hard to keep track of in the museum as they are in the average basement or attic, and individual trustees or staff members are likely to be whimsically playing house with collections. When somebody from your state attorney-general's office arrives to check on your museum's compliance with public trust statutes, you will need to be able to pull a file or click up a computer screen that identifies each object you have, tells where it is, summarizes what is known about it, specifies where and how you got it and under what conditions, and tells what shape it is in, what conservation treatment it needs or has been given, and what uses you have made of it to date, including in exhibits.

Because museums differ, no one collections policy should absolutely duplicate any other. At the minimum, however, each museum's policy should spell out rules for acquisitions (i.e., for accepting gifts and loaned objects and for making purchases), for deaccessioning (i.e., for removing objects in any way from the museum's collections), and for control of collections (i.e., for arrangements for their registration, care, and use). Ideally, a collections policy would cover all the following:

- Acquisition policies and procedures

- Documentation and care procedures

- Loan and borrowing provisions

- Security and insurance coverage

- Access and disclosure commitments and conditions

- Ethics to be observed by staff and trustees

- Deaccession rules

Once the collections-policy document establishes rules and procedures, then the collecting plan described earlier may go forward. Be sure to document each gift so that you can verify your ownership of an object and rights to its use, if any question arises. A simple certificate of gift will serve the purpose (see document F).

"Okay, fine," you may be saying, "obviously we need collections to do exhibits, so we'll devise a collections policy, a certificate of gift, and a collecting plan. Now can we go on to *exhibits?*"

You may, unless you want to be sure first that the objects you put into your exhibits do not crumble, fade, rust, warp, or otherwise disintegrate before your eyes and those of your visitors. That is what will happen if you do not also add to your plan provisions for *conservation.*

Conservation, too, you will remember from chapter 1, is an ongoing function, because whether your collections are in storage, being studied, on exhibit, or otherwise in use, they need protection from insects and rodents, from extremes of and fluctuations in temperature and humidity, from excessive levels of light, from airborne pollutants, from deliberate or inadvertent vandalism, and from any of a number of other things, depending on the materials of which the artifact is made. Because artifacts are different in the care they require and because repairs and protective treatments can themselves be damaging if ordinary household methods are followed rather than professionally established conservation techniques, a conservation program can be difficult for the nonprofessional to plan. You may need to seek planning help from a competent consultant.

The professional you hire to direct your museum, or any experienced museum person you engage as a consultant, should be able to help you plan good, overall protective conditions for your collections, including methods and procedures for evaluating the physical condition of each object when you get it and then periodically thereafter, particularly before and after you have used it in an exhibit or program. If your museum becomes big enough, your collections may warrant and your budget may permit hiring a trained professional conservator for your staff. But at least in the beginning, other arrangements can be made for expert treatment of objects in your collection that are in bad condition or in danger of rapid deterioration. Large museums in your area may have scientific conservators who can help, or you may seek assistance from one of several regional conservation centers (identified at the end of chapter 2). Your state museum association or state historical society probably can identify other qualified conservators near you. Some trained conservators are independent practitioners, who are available for examination and treatment jobs.

"Very well," you say, "my museum will identify in its plan the kind of expert conservation evaluation and activity it will need to protect its collections. So now, can we go on to exhibits?"

Yes, fine—if you can answer the following additional questions. Can you prove that the paintings you will put up on your museum wall are genuinely the work of the artists to which you attribute them? Are you sure that the bones you are displaying as a prehistoric mastodon's are not those of some oversized and more recent mule? Can you explain to visitors how butterflies like those mounted in your collection live, reproduce, and relate to the rest of their environment? And what changes did trolley cars, like the one you plan to display in your museum, produce in the social and economic development of your city?

In short, do you really understand the objects you plan to exhibit?

To keep your museum from simply spreading trivia or misinformation, please also plan for a program of ongoing *research.* Research means asking owners or donors everything they know about an object in preparation for its coming into the museum, then checking that information against other sources. It means documenting the basic facts about what an object is, while also studying its historical, artistic, or scientific context—the larger picture into which the object fits and which illuminates its significance. It means proving that your museum's old rifle really is a .45-caliber Springfield used in the U.S. Army after the Civil War. It also means finding out what this kind of weapon had to do with the outcome of battles in the wars between the U.S. Army and Native Americans and in the development of military technology.

Neither research nor collections themselves are very useful, of course, unless they are organized for retrieval. That is, each object in your collections, and all the information you have on it, needs to be accessible so that you can find it when you need it for an exhibit, a research report, or an educational program. This requires organizing information on items in collections by categories, so that when you need to know something about the guns in your collection, for example, you can find it under "Firearms," under products made by the "Springfield Armory," or under artifacts associated with the "Plains Indian Wars."

Museums now have generally replaced their card catalogues with computer files for storing and retrieving information on their collections. Computer cataloguing systems are available, but before developing a catalogue electronically, new museums would be wise to consult with those that have been through computerization. Whether manually or electronically, museums typically maintain separate accession files, donor files, and object files. Examples of forms and different systems for registering and cataloguing museum objects, electronically as well as manually, can be found in established museums and in books such as those cited at the end of this chapter.

Your plan needs to specify who will do research and cataloguing. Will it be members of the staff? A research committee of volunteers or of board members? Expert professors from local colleges or universities? Students under the supervision of teachers or museum staff? Also, you need to plan research facilities in your museum, such as a library of reference materials related to your collections. And remember that research needs to be continuous: new facts will turn up, new approaches will arise, new insights will become possible, and older interpretations will need review for possible revision.

Now at last, having planned for ongoing, behind-the-scenes requirements, you are almost ready for exhibits. Almost, because exhibits are only part of the public pay-off you are now ready to plan. Exhibits are one vehicle for a continuing activity called *interpretation*. Interpretation, essentially, is what you say about your museum's collections, in person and in writing, to help your public learn from and appreciate them. You may plan to interpret through several coordinated means of reaching the public.

Think of yourself as a member of that public living near a museum with a multifaceted interpretive program. You probably encounter museum interpretation without even going to the museum. Listening to the radio on the way home from work one day, you hear a fascinating discussion about life in an earlier era in your community. The program is part of a series of weekly broadcasts produced by your community's museum. Stopping at the shopping center, you find a storefront exhibit of the kinds of things that a general store would have offered its customers in your city twenty-five, fifty, or a hundred years ago, accompanied by easy-to-understand information about developments in merchandising and consumerism, compliments of the community museum. Reaching home, you turn on the television and somebody in an educational program is showing different kinds of early-day farm implements from the collections of the museum and explaining how they changed agricultural production. In the evening newspaper, you find an article by the museum director about an excellent artist whose watercolor landscapes of your area have been acquired by the museum.

Suddenly, you are interrupted by your eleven-year-old son, who wants to tell you all about the special trip his fifth-grade class took by bus that day. Where? To the museum. "We learned about all kinds of animals from around here! Do you know that we used to have real buffalo? Do you know how to tell poisonous from nonpoisonous snakes? Do you know how birds are able to fly?" Which reminds you, isn't somebody scheduled to speak about the area's ecology at Rotary or the Garden Club this week? Somebody from the museum?

What is this museum that seems to pop up with interesting information in so many ways? You get on the Internet and check its website, where you discover it has a lot of attractive programs. And there on the Web, you take a virtual tour of its exhibits, which look so interesting that you decide to go see them for real. Today, a museum without an attractive website is missing an almost indispensable means both of publicizing itself and of reaching the public with its exhibits and educational offerings. You will see how museums are using websites by clicking on website links provided by the Museum Computer Network (www.mcn.edu), which is dedicated to fostering the cultural aims of museums through the use of computer technology.

So the next Saturday you take your family to visit the museum. At the entrance, a person gives you a brochure that tells about what is on exhibit in the building and where. This person also asks if you would like a guided tour, available in half an hour. Or you may rent a device with a recording and ear phones so that you can hear about objects you are seeing as you walk through the exhibits. First, if you like, you may sit in the museum's theater and see an audiovisual program about the history of the community, made from the museum's collection of old photographs, or a program about the other kinds of things it exhibits.

Nearby, you notice an alcove where the museum sells publications, which look fascinating. There is an illustrated history of your community published by the museum. There are catalogues depicting different special exhibits that the museum has presented. There are copies of the museum's regular newsletter, containing articles about new objects in the museum's collections, along with announcements of lectures, films, and other special programs.

Publications, audiovisual productions, guided tours, self-guiding tours, lectures, films, school programs, presentations to community groups, traveling exhibits, newspaper articles, programs on radio and television, website resources—all of these can be parts of the museum's overall interpretive program, and you, the visitor, have not even reached the exhibits yet!

Planning interpretive activities means deciding which of the many possible devices your museum wants to use to extend the educational reach of your collections. Also, you may plan to coordinate these devices with each other, publishing catalogues when you open new exhibits, for example, or creating traveling displays to meet curricular needs of school programs. As for exhibits, some can be what museum people call *permanent*, such as those that tell the basic story of your community, and others can be temporary, such as a six-month special show on some particular group, event, or facet of history, art, or nature in your region. And from time to time you may plan to bring in traveling exhibits from other museums as well. You may then even plan receptions for new exhibit openings!

Exhibit preparation itself, however, like every one of the other interpretive activities named earlier, takes special planning. It is an art, requiring imaginative combinations of artifacts with well-written labels, appropriate graphic material, and attractive layouts or showcases. Some exhibits may include film clips and educational components using interactive computers. Sound, light, and color all can enhance the effect of an exhibit. But unless sensitively handled, these things also can detract from the exhibit by overwhelming the artifacts, the originals, the "real things." Too much information or poorly designed glitz can overwhelm visitors. Museum curators and educators plan with great care the content of exhibits, recognizing that museum visitors differ in age, in attention span, in learning style, in education, in interests, and in perspectives. Exhibits do not need to reduce objects to illustrating large panels of text ("books on walls") or subordinate them to some single, didactically explicated "story line." Museum objects need interpretation or context to varying degrees, in varying ways. They can be approached from multiple points of view, including the visitor's, particularly if the museum's interactive devices offer exploratory options.

Developing exhibits may be the last part of your museum plan to be implemented. However, a curator, exhibit designer, and relevant scholars should be involved in the exhibit-development process as soon as possible. You might consider offering some temporary, introductory kinds of exhibits to whet the interest of your public as you get the rest of the museum's programs in place. But do not forget the multiple other ways for sharing and interpreting your collections, or the collecting, conservation, and research that are essential for you to have anything significant to interpret. You now know that programming of any kind requires answering these four questions in your basic museum-planning checklist:

9. What will be your collections policy?
10. What conservation needs must you meet and how?
11. What provisions will you make for ongoing research?
12. What interpretive methods will you use to reach your publics?

For More Information

On collection accessioning and registration, the following may be useful:

- American Association of Museums (AAM), *Gifts of Property: A Guide for Donors and Museums*, 2nd ed., AAM, 2002

- Blackaby, James R., and Patricia Greeno, *The Revised Nomenclature for Museum Cataloging: A Revised and Expanded Version of Robert G. Chenhall's System for Classifying Manmade Objects*, AASLH/AltaMira Press, 1988

- Buck, Rebecca A., and Jean Allman Gilmore, *The New Museum Registration Methods*, 4th ed., AAM, 1998

- Malero, Marie C., *A Legal Primer on Managing Museum Collections*, 2nd ed., Smithsonian Institution Press, 1998

- Reibel, Daniel B., *Registration Methods for the Small Museum*, AASLH/AltaMira Press, 1997

On conservation and preservation, the following may be useful:

- AAM, *Caring for Collections*, AAM, 1984.

- Applebaum, Barbara, *Guide to Environmental Protection of Collections*, Sound View Press, 1991

- Fahy, Anne, *Collections Management*, Routledge, 1994
- Knell, Simon, *Care of Collections*, Routledge, 1994
- Layne, Steven P., *The Cultural Property Protection Manual*, Layne Consultants International, 2002
- MacLeish, A. Bruce, *The Care of Antiques and Historical Collections*, 2nd ed., AASLH/AltaMira Press, 1985
- Schultz, Arthur W., ed., *Caring for Your Collections*, U.S. National Committee to Save America's Cultural Collection/Heritage Preservation, 1992
- Zycherman, L., *A Guide to Museum Pest Control*, Association of Systematic Collections, 1988

Also on conservation, the American Institute for Conservation of Historic and Artistic Works (http://aic.stanford.edu) has individual brochures on caring for architecture, books, ceramics, glass objects, art works, furniture, videotapes, metal objects, photos, and textiles and *Guidelines for Selecting a Conservator.*

Also, the following technical leaflets and video from the American Association for State and Local History (AASLH) are pertinent to conservation:

- *Basic Deterioration and Preventative Measures for Museum Collections* (video 482VT)
- *Collections Care: What to Do When You Can't Afford to Do Anything* (198)
- *Conserving Local Archival Materials on a Limited Budget* (86)
- *Exhibit Conservation: Strategies for Producing a Preservation-Responsible Exhibition* (215)
- *Historic Landscapes and Gardens: Procedures for Restoration* (199)
- *A Holistic Approach to Museum Pest Management* (171)
- *Management of Firearms Collections* (136)

On historic house preservation, the following are useful:

- Andrews, Carol, et al., *Coping with Contamination: A Primer for Preservationists*, National Trust for Historic Preservation, 1993

- Butcher-Younghans, Sherry, *Historic House Museums: A Practical Handbook for Their Care, Preservation, and Management*, Oxford University Press, 1996

- Chitty, Gill, and David Baker, eds., *Managing Historic Sites and Buildings: Balancing Presentation and Preservation*, Routledge, 1999

- Heaver, Melissa, *Housekeeping for Historic Homes and House Museums*, National Trust for Historic Preservation, 2000

- Tri-State Coalition of Historic Places, *Standards and Practices for Historic Site Administration*, Tri-State Coalition of Historic Places, 2000

- Whelchel, Harriet, *Caring for Your Historic House*, Heritage Preservation and the National Park Service, Harry N. Abrams, Inc., 1998

- Zagars, Julie, ed., *Preservation Yellow Pages*, John Wiley and Sons/Preservation Press, 1997

Also, the following technical leaflets from AASLH are pertinent to historic house care:

- *Before Restoration Begins: Keeping Your Historic House Intact* (67)

- *The Eight Most Common Mistakes in Restoring Houses* (118)

- *Log Cabin Restoration* (74)

On museum research activities, the following is useful, along with works on local history research listed at the end of chapter 2:

- Yeide, Nancy H., et al., *The AAM Guide to Provenance Research*, AAM, 2001

Also, the following technical leaflets from AASLH are pertinent to museum research:

- *Documentation Practices in Historical Collections* (176)
- *The History of a House: How to Trace It* (89)

On various kinds of museum interpretation, the following are useful:

- AAM, *Museum Visitor Services Manual*, AAM Resource Report, 2001
- Alderson, William T., and Shirley Payne Low, *Interpretation of Historic Sites*, 2nd ed., AASLH/AltaMira Press, 1985
- Anderson, Jay, ed., *Living History Reader*, vol. 1, *Museums*, AASLH/AltaMira Press, 1991
- Brochu, Lisa, *Interpretive Planning: The 5-M Model for Successful Planning Projects*, National Association for Interpretation/InterpPress, 2003
- Brochu, Lisa, and Tim Merriman, *Connecting Your Audience to Heritage Resources*, National Association for Interpretation/InterpPress, 2002
- Donnelly, Jessica Foy, ed., *Interpreting Historic House Museums*, AASLH/AltaMira Press, 2002
- Garvin, Victoria, ed., *Exemplary Interpretation: Seminar Sourcebook*, AAM, 2001
- Kaufman, Polly Welts, and Katharine T. Corbett, *Her Past around Us: Interpreting Sites for Women's History*, Krieger, 2003
- Levy, Barbara Abramoff, et al., *Great Tours! Thematic Tours and Guide Training for Historic Sites*, AASLH/AltaMira Press, 2002
- Rios-Bustamante, Antonio, and Christine Marin, *Latinos in Museums: A Heritage Reclaimed*, Krieger, 1998

- Sachatello-Sawyer, Bonnie, et al., *Adult Museum Programs: Designing Meaningful Experiences*, AASLH/AltaMira Press, 2002

Also, the following technical leaflet and videos from AASLH are pertinent to museum interpretation:

- *Deciding What to Interpret* (video 470VT)
- *Interpretive Design* (video 471VT)
- *Interpreting History through Pictorial Documents* (video 472VT)
- *Interpreting History through Three-Dimensional Objects* (video 473VT)
- *Interpreting History through Written Documents* (video 474VT)
- *Labels: Verbal Communications of the Interpretive Message* (video 476VT)
- *Seven Ways to Look at an Artifact* (91)
- *Successful Interpretive Planning* (video 480VT)

On exhibits, the following are useful:

- Ames, Kenneth, et al., eds., *Ideas and Images: Developing Interpretive History Exhibits*, AASLH/AltaMira Press, 1991
- Belcher, Michael, *Exhibitions in Museums*, Smithsonian Institution Press, 1992
- Caulton, Tim, *Hands-On Exhibitions: Managing Interactive Museums and Science Centres*, Routledge, 1998
- Lord, Barry, and Gail Dexter Lord, *The Manual of Museum Exhibitions*, AltaMira Press, 2001
- McLean, Kathleen, *Planning for People in Museum Exhibitions*, Association of Science-Technology Centers, 1993

- Serrell, Beverly, *Exhibit Labels: An Interpretive Approach*, AltaMira Press, 1996

Also, the following technical leaflets from AASLH are pertinent to exhibits:

- *Planning Exhibits: From Concept to Completion* (137)
- *A Systemized Approach to Exhibit Production Management* (175)

On traveling and temporary exhibits, the following are useful:

- Freeman, Ruth, and Paul Martinovich, *The Evolution of an Exhibit: Community Museums and Travelling Exhibits*, Ontario Museum Association, 2001
- Howarth, Shirley Reiff, ed., *Guide to Traveling Exhibition Organizers*, The Humanities Exchange, Inc., 2000
- Witteborg, Lothar P., *Good Show! A Practical Guide to Temporary Exhibitions*, 2nd ed., Smithsonian Institution Traveling Exhibition Service, 1991

On interpretive education and school programs, the following are useful:

- Falk, John H., and Lynn D. Dierking, *Learning from Museums: Visitor Experiences and the Making of Meaning*, AASLH/AltaMira Press, 2000
- Falk, John H., and Lynn D. Dierking, *Lessons without Limit: How Free-Choice Learning Is Transforming Education*, AltaMira Press, 2002
- Grinder, Alison T., and Sue McCoy, *The Good Guide: A Sourcebook for Interpreters*, Ironwood Publishing, 1985
- Hein, George E., *Learning in the Museum*, Routledge, 1998
- Moffat, Hazel, and Vicky Woollard, eds., *Museum and Gallery Education: A Manual of Good Practice*, AltaMira Press, 2000

- Sheppard, Beverly, ed., *Building Museum and School Partnerships*, AAM/Pennsylvania Federation of Museums and Historical Organizations, 1993

Also, the following technical leaflets and video from AASLH are pertinent to museum education:

- *Developing Effective Educational Programs* (202)

- *Museum Education: A Tool of Interpretation* (video 479VT)

- *Planning Museum Tours for School Groups* (93)

On interpretation through publications, media, and the Internet, the following are useful:

- Greenwood, Lara, *The Basics of Designing a Museum Web Site*, 1998, www.peabody.harvard.edu/webbasics

- Kebabian, Helen, and William Padgett, *Production of Museum Publications: A Step-by-Step Guide*, The Exhibition Alliance, 1990

- Koelling, Jill Marie, *Digital Imaging: A Practical Approach*, AASLH/AltaMira Press, 2004

- Mintz, Ann, and Selma Thomas, *The Virtual and the Real: Media in the Museum*, AAM, 1998

- Perkins, John, *Planning for Museum Automation*, published for the Museum Computer Network by Archives and Museum Informatics as #17 in AMI's Technical Reports series

- Still, Julie M., ed., *Creating Web-Accessible Databases: Case Studies for Libraries, Museums, and Other Nonprofits*, Information Today, Inc., 2001

Also, the following technical leaflet from AASLH is pertinent to collections management:

- *Digitizing Your Collection* (217)

The Plantation Life Gallery. The gallery is part of the Alexander & Baldwin Sugar Museum in Puunene, Maui, Hawaii, which documents the sugar industry and its multiethnic work force. Photo by Gaylord Kubota. Courtesy of the Alexander & Baldwin Sugar Museum.

9

Recruit the Human Resources

Your planning outline is nearly complete. The last chapter dealt with ongoing needs of your museum for collections management, conservation, research, and multiple forms of interpretation, including exhibition. Completing the plan requires providing for competent people to carry out these activities. What human resources will your program plans require? And on what schedule? For time, too, is a resource.

For example, you might set up a three-year plan, culminating in the public opening of your museum. In the first year, you might concentrate money and effort on the preparation of your physical facilities so that a protective environment and adequate, well-equipped work spaces will be ready for your collections. In the second year, you might start meeting major objectives of your collecting or acquisitions plan and your research or documentation plan, along with attending to conservation as artifacts come in. Your interpretive program, including exhibits, might then get the major focus in the third year. Your fundraising, staff hiring, and training of volunteers would be phased in as needed.

However, if your community is too impatient to let you prepare everything before going public, or your fund-raising requires an early demonstration of benefits, you might have to open some temporary exhibits or start some programs for schools or outside groups at the same time that you carry out backstage preparations for a larger program, just to show everyone that something really is happening at the new museum. That may mean planning to raise money and to recruit personnel on a faster schedule than you had intended. Either way, timing should be specified within your plan, preferably with specific assignments and deadlines for committees and individuals.

Whatever you do, someone needs to be put in overall charge of activities almost from the start. The earlier your museum's trustees or board members designate a director of operations or executive director or chief executive officer, the better. Ideally, this director will participate in the planning as well as take day-to-day responsibility for carrying out the plan. At the latest, the engagement of a director should come after the museum's purpose is adopted, the probability of community support is determined, an assessment is made of available collections and facilities, and the governing authority is established.

Museums have been developed and operated successfully by volunteer directors—at least by volunteers who were willing and able to learn a lot of concepts and skills quickly and make effective use of outside expertise. But hiring a qualified, paid professional director will give you the advantage of direction by someone with training and experience. It makes no more sense to turn over a community museum to an inexperienced volunteer to manage than it would to turn over the local health clinic or public library to an untrained person. In fact, the salary of your community's library director or school principal is a reasonable guide to what your museum director should be paid, at least if your plans call for a museum of comparable budget size. Information on museum staff salaries may be available from your state museum or historical society, or from your regional or state museum association. Even if you must begin without a paid, experienced museum professional, you should plan for the support of professional staff eventually.

When you can seek a professional museum director, procedures for conducting a search and evaluating applicants are similar to such procedures for other kinds of professionals. City and county governments will, of course, use their regular, established personnel procedures in seeking employees for a publicly supported museum. Otherwise, unless your museum's governing board itself is small, the board should designate no more than a half-dozen persons as a search committee to invite and evaluate applications for the director position. Some museum boards engage professional "headhunters," firms that specialize in helping organizations find suitable executives, and they can be well worth their fees, particularly if the museum you plan will be large enough to warrant a far-reaching search for a highly qualified veteran of museum work.

In any case, the board, search committee, or responsible government official should write in plain language a realistic description of the job (see document E for an example) and of the qualifications considered necessary and desirable. Professionals in your state historical society, museum, or museum association can help you determine these competencies. Then you can advertise the position in the classified employment-opportunity sections of newspapers that have wide enough distribution and of museum association periodicals, such as *Aviso* and *Dispatch*, published by the American Association of Museums (AAM) and the American Association for State and Local History (AASLH), respectively. These publications are where professionals tend to look for job opportunities.

Also, it can help to send copies of the job description and requirements to directors of established museums in your state or region, with a request that they call the position to the attention of any professional they know who might be interested and qualified. But do not rely exclusively on word-of-mouth or "the old-boy network." Advertising openly gives you the opportunity to consider good candidates who otherwise will not receive word about the position. You will also expand your pool of good candidates, as well as comply with applicable laws, by advertising that you are an equal-opportunity employer.

You may also wish to send your position description to universities that have training programs in museum studies, public history, cultural resource management, or arts, science, or historical administration. Universities offering such courses often keep in touch with their graduates and provide job-placement services. A directory of training programs in museum studies, historic preservation, public history, and nonprofit management is maintained by the Smithsonian Center for Education and Museum Studies (http://museumstudies.si.edu/traindirect.htm). Also, you may get insight into the adequacy for your museum of the training a program provides or an applicant has received by consulting a book entitled *Graduate Training in Museum Studies: What Students Need to Know,* by Marjorie Schwarzer (AAM, 2001).

The job advertisement should include information on the salary range you can offer, fringe benefits, required and desirable skills and experience, principal responsibilities, the closing date for submitting applications, the address to which applications should be sent, and assurance that the museum is an equal-opportunity employer. The search committee should respond to every applicant, acknowledging receipt of each application and giving the applicant an idea of when to expect to hear further.

The search committee should determine which applicants seem best for the job on paper and then request references from those applicants—statements from previous employers or others who can comment knowledgeably on the experience, abilities, and character of applicants. The most promising applicants whose references prove supportive should then be invited to come to your community for an interview, at the expense of the museum board. Before they come, you should provide them background information about the museum's plans, preferably including the museum's governing document and mission statement, and the community or groups it will serve. Ask each candidate to come separately to meet with the search committee extensively and with other board members or the entire board at least casually and to see museum facilities or collections that you already may have.

After completing the interviews, the search committee may want to ask applicants for additional information or references. If by then no candidate stands out, but more than one seems potentially satisfactory, these "short-list" applicants may be invited for a second interview, this time with the entire board. In any event, the full board or other governing body of the museum should make the final decision after a recommendation from the search committee. And when the board approves a candidate—preferably unanimously—the board chairperson or president should negotiate with the successful candidate the terms for a contract letter that will specify salary, fringe benefits, duties, expectations, extent and limits of authority, length of appointment, standards and procedures for performance evaluation, and procedures to follow if termination should be desired by either party. Given the current ambiguity surrounding legal rights of employees, advance review of employment agreements by legal counsel for the museum is advisable. Applicants who do not make the short list should receive tactful notice right away. Finalists may be notified after acceptance of the position, preferably by signed contract, by the winning candidate. Poor treatment of professionals you do *not* hire could adversely affect the reputation your museum gets in the field.

When, and only when, an employment agreement has been concluded with a director, public announcement should be made. A press release to newspapers and radio and television stations in your area about the new director should be part of general publicity plans for the museum's development. And when the new director arrives, a welcoming reception can be helpful, to which—ideally—you would invite everyone in the community who is likely to be of help as the museum gets going. The new director will need to become a publicly recognizable representative of the new museum and will need the board's help to get acquainted in the community.

The museum development plan you work out with the director will determine whether you will need and can afford to hire additional paid staff, at full- or part-time salary. No staff positions should be created without authorization from the board in long-range plans and annual budgets, but once a position is authorized and budgeted, the staff director should have authority to fill it, not the board. This includes filling unpaid positions and engaging volunteers. A staff director cannot be held responsible for staff performance without having authority to select the staff.

Almost all museums, no matter how many paid professional staff members they have, also use volunteers to carry out valuable, sometimes essential, functions. Under proper supervision, volunteers can help with almost anything—guiding tours through the museum's exhibits, taking tickets, helping with research, keeping records, or providing accounting services, legal counsel, and fund-raising leadership. Your plan should designate what parts of your programs can be carried out with the help of volunteers, so that provision can be made for recruiting and preparing them. Successful museums treat volunteers with as much care and respect as professional staff, which includes having high expectations of them. Many museums have a director of volunteers, who recruits and trains unpaid staff members and supervises their work.

It can be as useful to have job descriptions for volunteers as for paid staff. Volunteers who merely wander in off the street should not automatically be accepted. All candidates for volunteer work need to be interviewed concerning experience, abilities, and interests, and each may legitimately be asked to provide references to check for such qualities as dependability and honesty. In accepting a volunteer, the museum should put on paper an agreement specifying what the volunteer will do, how many hours will be worked per week, and at what times of the day or night the individual will be on the premises. Volunteers must be given work that is meaningful and satisfying to them as well as useful to the museum. Once they agree to do certain things, however, they need to understand that the museum will depend on that. Volunteers who persistently come late or not at all, who do not follow directions for their duties, or who interfere with other staff should be tactfully dismissed, just as paid staff should be dismissed in cases of inadequate performance, unreliability, and insubordination.

Training for volunteers is essential and takes time and resources for which your museum's long-range plan and annual budgets should provide. A retired school teacher may have great experience for conducting visitors through a historic house museum three afternoons a week, but that individual needs to receive information about the house, the length of the tour, ways to deal with special questions and problem situations, and insight into the relationship of the volunteer's work to the museum's mission and its activities overall. Moreover, tours given by docents should be monitored from time to time and evaluated. To be accepted, volunteers should agree to evaluations and to keep their work at high standards of performance. Treating volunteer work as the genuinely important element it is can enhance the satisfaction that good volunteers get from it—and the effort they put into it. Those who perform well should be rewarded with recognition by the professional staff and the board.

Planning the use of human resources includes providing for training. That is, as the museum develops, its paid and volunteer staff members will need opportunities to improve their skills and understanding. They may find such opportunities through memberships in museum associations whose publications keep them abreast of the museum field—magazines, newsletters, technical reports, books, and material accessible on websites. Provision should be made as well to send professional staff and volunteers to occasional workshops and seminars offered by museum organizations and to annual meetings of state, regional, or national associations that serve the field. Such meetings not only offer instructive formal presentations in their programs, but also enable museum workers to get acquainted with peers, share ideas with people dealing with similar problems and organizations, and learn where to find help when special needs arise through the year. Getting away to an instructive meeting of one kind or another from time to time is a great way to make helpful contacts, widen one's outlook, and recharge one's energy and enthusiasm. Your plan for staffing each of the museum's programs should not only describe jobs and the number of people needed, volunteer and paid, but also should define the kinds and levels of expertise they will need and how the museum will develop their abilities.

Additionally, training needs to include attention to museum ethics. Some ethical standards adopted by museums are not unique to them. For example, museums, like other organizations, consider it unethical for a board member or employee to provide preferential treatment in exchange for gifts that constitute bribes from outside bidders, contractors, and influence seekers. Museums, like other organizations, have ethical prohibitions against sexual harassment, racial discrimination, and favoritism in promotion. Museums also join other organizations in expecting employees—and trustees—to act on behalf of the museum only within established procedural rules for organizational decision making and implementation.

Some ethical considerations are more specific to museums. These include rules to which earlier chapters alluded, such as prohibitions against providing donors with inflated collection appraisals, competing with one's own museum by collecting in the same field, and arbitrarily disposing of or making personal use of museum collections.

Museums also, especially recently, are struggling with more complex ethical requirements. Ethical museums take steps to be sure that objects they purchase or accept have not been stolen or obtained through illicit trade. Ethical museums whose collections contain human skeletal remains and objects sacred to certain cultures treat such objects with dignity or transfer them in response to legitimate claims. And ethical museums are attempting to clarify how much and what kinds of publicity, including naming rights, they will and will not give to commercial and individual donors who provide support for exhibitions and facilities.

Even the newest and smallest museums need ethical guidelines, which yours can develop by consulting codes of ethical conduct issued by museum associations and professional groups. Such codes are identified in listings at the end of this chapter. It is also wise to keep track of how the profession is dealing with ethical controversies and legal developments pertinent to museums, which you can do through magazines, newsletters, and websites of museum associations.

Now you understand some basic staffing and training requirements that must not be overlooked in planning a museum. So now you can answer the next four questions in your basic museum-planning checklist:

13. What time schedule for development will the museum follow?

14. Who will direct your museum and how will you recruit that person?

15. What staff positions, paid and volunteer, will be needed?

16. What provisions will you make for staff training in museum work and museum ethics?

For More Information

Concerning director recruitment and museum staffing, the following resources are useful:

- AAM, *Museum Job Descriptions and Organizational Charts*, AAM Resource Report, 1999

- Albert, Sheila, *Hiring the Chief Executive: A Practical Guide to the Search and Selection Process*, BoardSource, 2000

- Association of Art Museum Directors, *Model Museum Director's Employment Contract*, Association of Art Museum Directors, 1996

- Cutler, Charlene Perkins, *The Employer's Handbook: A Guide to Personnel Practices and Policies for Museums*, New England Museum Association, 1996

Concerning volunteer programs, the following are useful:

- *The Docent Handbook*, National Docent Symposium Council, 2001

- Ellis, Susan J., *The Volunteer Recruitment (and Membership Development) Book*, 3rd ed., Energize, Inc., 2002

- Fisher, James C., and Kathleen M. Cole, *Leadership and Management of Volunteer Programs*, Jossey-Bass, 1993

- Hall, Esther, *Investing in Volunteers: A Guide to Effective Volunteer Management*, National Trust for Historic Preservation, 1994

- Kuyper, Joan, *Volunteer Program Administration: A Handbook for Museums and Other Cultural Institutions*, American Association of Museum Volunteers, 1993

- Morrison, Emily Kittle, *Leadership Skills: Developing Volunteers for Organizational Success*, Fisher Books, 1994

- Wilson, Marlene, *The Effective Management of Volunteer Programs*, Volunteer Management Associates, 1976

The following technical leaflets from AASLH are pertinent to museum volunteers:

- *Establishing a Volunteer Program: A Case Study* (170)

- *Training Docents: How to Talk to Visitors* 125)

- *Student Projects and Internships in a Museum Setting* (184)

Two good examples of volunteer handbooks, developed by a specific museum for use with its volunteers, are available on request from the Texas Seaport Museum, Pier 21, No. 8, Galveston, TX, (409) 763-1877, kurt.voss@galvestonhistory.org.

Concerning museum personnel ethics, the following are useful:

- AAM, *Code of Ethics for Museums*, revised, AAM, 2000

- AAM, *Codes of Ethics and Practice of Interest to Museums*, AAM Resource Report, 2000

- AAM, *Writing a Museum Code of Ethics*, AAM Resource Report, 1993

- AASLH, *Statement of Professional Standards and Ethics*, AASLH, June 2003, www.aaslh.org/ethics.htm

- American Historical Association, *Statement on Standards for Professional Conduct, 2003 Edition*, American Historical Association, 2003

- Edson, Gary, *Museum Ethics,* Routledge, 1997
- National Council on Public History, *Ethical Guidelines for the Historian,* National Council on Public History, 1986, www.ncph.org/ethics.html
- World Federation of Friends of Museums, *Code of Ethics for Museum Friends and Volunteers,* World Federation of Friends of Museums, 1998

Elvehjem Museum of Art. The Elvehjem Museum of Art, affiliated with the University of Wisconsin, Madison, is one of many museums that serve academic communities. Photo courtesy of the Elvehjem Museum of Art, University of Wisconsin, Madison.

10

Now Will It Really Work?

Congratulations! You now know the rudiments of a museum development plan. And when you put such a plan into operation, you will have a wonderful museum, right? Maybe. Fast forward the reel for a moment to see what your museum may be like once in operation. Pretend that you are observing a big meeting of the board of your museum just after the end of its first or second fiscal year.

At the meeting, the carefully kept minutes of the board's last meeting are read by the secretary and approved. The treasurer reports that income for the year has covered expenses and that fund-raising goals have been met from all anticipated sources. The chair of the buildings and grounds committee certifies that scheduled repairs have been made in the museum building and that the local garden club has completed all the landscaping. The chair of the acquisitions committee reports that artifacts have so far been obtained on schedule to fill gaps in the collections. The director reports that all key staff positions are filled, training is being provided, and activities are on schedule; that the reference library is established and documentation has been completed for items to be used in the first exhibits; that they are ready to open; that objects not on exhibit are registered and organized in storage areas that meet acceptable standards for conservation; and that publications, school programs, and other interpretive activities are proceeding on a coordinated basis. The director of volunteers then announces that docents have been trained to conduct tours and help with research. The lawyer on the board reports that all documents are in order, including tax-exempt certification, a collections policy, and letters of agreement with staff and volunteers. Everything appears to be covered perfectly.

Sorry. There are still some important things missing. In Heaven, a plan may provide a perfect blueprint for what actually happens, but on earth, the best-made plans of mice and museums often go astray. Your museum will work well only if some persons not yet mentioned are present at this mythical meeting, persons whose participation will help you adjust to inevitable imperfections.

For example, there should be a report from an independent auditor, a certified public accountant (CPA), whom you hire (if a CPA firm will not volunteer services) to determine annually or at least regularly whether, in fact, the museum's financial report can be relied on. The audit firm will prepare an objective, written opinion on whether your financial statements present fairly the financial position of your organization in terms of assets and liabilities on its balance sheet and income and expenses on its activity statement (in business, this is called the profit and loss statement). The audit may also cover other financial statements, such as a report on the museum's uses of cash, to see that everything is in accordance with generally accepted accounting principles. This independent check on the museum's financial practices is important not only to the board, but also to potential donors.

In actual practice, you are also likely to have a report from the secretary of the board on amendments that have been proposed to the bylaws or even to the museum's constitution. Such documents need periodic review and may require changes, at least occasionally, or the addition of provisions to cover unanticipated issues. Records of such changes need to be kept carefully and reported to the Internal Revenue Service to protect your tax-exempt status.

Also, at this point you will need a report from the museum's director or the chair of the publicity committee explaining what is being done—and with what degree of success so far—to arouse and sustain public interest in using the museum. It is quite possible to develop a technically wonderful museum entirely according to plan, only to discover one flaw: in spite of expectations, nobody comes to it. This will happen if no one effectively tells the public about it.

Indeed, is anybody present at this hypothetical meeting from outside the museum? Where are representatives of *stakeholders*, as they are often called—groups outside the museum who work with or have interests in it? Where are teachers who have been collaborating with your museum on school programs? Where are representatives of other communities for which you are providing traveling exhibits? Where are major contributors of collections or funds who deserve to be publicly recognized? Where are politicians who have been sympathetic to your cause? And where are people from different groups within your community who can give you feedback on how well connected you are with the feelings and interests of all major segments of your potential audience?

Not all such people should necessarily be invited to routine board meetings, but the museum is incomplete without keeping them, one way or another, informed about and involved in the museum's activities. If such people begin to feel ignored, left out, or unrewarded, you will certainly eventually have visitors at your meetings—angry ones who may not have been expected, let alone invited. Maintaining political and public connections and communication is a continuing museum requirement.

Moreover, what means has the museum organization, itself, set up to evaluate its programs, now that they are in place? Suppose that school students do not actually learn what you thought your exhibits, guides, and educational materials were so wonderfully designed to teach them? What if the adult public mostly stands around in front of your carefully prepared exhibits and yawns? What happens if people in large segments of your community do not show up because they feel they will not be wanted or that your programs are irrelevant to their interests and cultures?

It is helpful to keep track of the numbers of people who visit your museum, participate in its programs, and click on its website. But such statistics do not say a lot about the *quality* of what

visitors find or the meaningfulness of the experience you provide. Have you planned to use questionnaires or interviews with
visitors to see what they value in your offerings and what they
do not? Are they coming away feeling that they have had the
kind of experience you intend and appreciate it? The audience
research recommended in chapter 3 as part of planning should
continue after the museum is operational.

Evaluation is difficult and you cannot make every visitor
stop at the exit door and take a test. But unless you solicit some
kind of feedback, you will have no indication of how well you
are meeting your public-benefit goals, and you will not know
what may need improvement in the future. Nor will you be able
to provide evidence to major funders, grant makers, and other
potential donors that, on the one hand, you are effective, or on
the other, that you genuinely need help to make specific im-
provements.

Alas, this is still not all. Even after implementing your
plan, you will want to hear reports from your planning committee. This is because your plan will need regular review and
revision in light of things you did not know would happen.
Plans need to be adjusted to accommodate opportunities and
obstacles that you did not foresee as well as successes and dis-
appointments in what you planned to do. If your fund-raising
drive nets twice what you estimated, clearly you have options
for expanding or accelerating your previous plans. Con-
versely, you will be forced to reduce them if fund-raising falls
short. Also, you have to adjust for what you cannot control—
inflationary hikes in your operating costs, for example, or
losses of income in financial recessions. Clearly, you cannot
proceed on your plan's original assumptions if a major acquisition turns out to cost much more than you thought, if a major financial supporter backs out, if a donor withdraws a collection offer, or if a tornado rips off the museum's roof.
Effective planning includes both contingency and emergency
planning.

A plan, after all, is a guideline for reaching objectives based
on reasonable assumptions in the present about the future. Plans
need to be reviewed at least annually, preferably quarterly, and

in some instances even monthly, to see whether objectives are being met on schedule and within budget, and if not, why not. Financial reports should be produced and reviewed every month, or, for small museums, at least quarterly.

Also, planning needs to be extended regularly. Each year the long-range plan should be added to by at least one additional year, so that your plan is always looking well ahead. Thus, planning is a regular, ongoing museum function, not a one-time, upfront activity.

Attention to these matters will help give you a well-developed museum organization capable of coping with change and the vagaries of an unpredictable world. At your meeting, an audit report certifies the soundness of your financial statements, but advises the tightening of some of your financial controls. The board's secretary recommends bylaw changes to make one of the governing procedures less cumbersome and the board-member nominating process more open to people from underrepresented segments of your community. Your publicity committee makes clear that the public's participation in your museum's activities is not being taken for granted. The board discusses the significance of information presented by the director from a spot survey of museum visitors, or prospective visitors, about their expectations and reactions. And a teacher gives the board fresh perspective on what is desired from the museum within the school curriculum. Additionally, the director or planning committee chair proposes changes in the long-range plan that will enable the museum to continue on its mission but cope with significant change.

At the end of that meeting, you will truly deserve congratulations. You will then have an impressive museum operation. And you will have done it by answering these final four questions in your basic museum-planning checklist:

17. How will you cope with change?

18. How will you conduct ongoing planning?

19. How will you evaluate your museum's activities?

20. How will you keep your museum alive, dynamic, creative, even visionary, and closely connected to your community?

Please consider a parting word about that last question.

In stations in the London Underground, there used to be a colorful advertisement for museums—a big poster—with this message on it, "Local museums are treasure houses where unlikely objects—curious, ingenious, comic, even beautiful—lie stranded for our gaze. They indicate local pride and a sense of identity. More vividly evocative of the everyday past than our grander institutions, they deserve and reward our notice."

"Stranded" is hardly the right word, particularly if you put into a museum all the care that has been outlined in this book. But how true the rest of the description can be! And how useful to remember, after reviewing so many technical considerations, that the intent of it all is to produce a "treasure house" of one kind or another. Determining what to treasure, caring for things that we treasure, and explaining why we treasure them is the essential mission of museums, whether we pursue it through scientific description, aesthetic appreciation, or intellectual education. Remember also that we may not always know why an ancient spear point, the bones of an extinct animal, the wagon of an early settler, a document written by someone famous, a face in a photograph, or a particular painting so captures our imaginations that it remains meaningful in our lives long after we have seen it in a museum. We know only that all the effort it takes to make a museum work well is worthwhile if visiting that museum gives pleasure, arouses emotions, stimulates thought, and otherwise produces memorable experiences. Doing all the technical things right is only a means to that end.

So, there you have it. If this book has done its job, you now know the basics of your job as a museum planner. And you know how demanding, difficult, and complex successful museum development can be. In closing, consider a real-life example of the possible rewards of your effort.

Almost as far south as you can get in the state of Texas, just across the Rio Grande from Mexico, is a place that many visitors to the Smithsonian probably never heard of: Edinburg, Texas, population 48,465 in the 2000 census. It is the seat of Hidalgo County, whose 569,463 residents are fewer than the number of people, on average, who in 2002 visited the Smithsonian Institution's museums, zoo, and traveling exhibits in a single week. But that relatively small community has developed a museum of impressive vitality and viability.

The Hidalgo County Historical Museum opened its doors in April 1970 after six years of careful planning and preparation. The work began in 1964, when a county survey committee prepared for a regional museum "in order that present and future generations will not only know the significance of the rich traditions of South Texas and Northern Mexico, but learn from the past" and recognize "the need to preserve this historical heritage which has been bestowed upon them." The peoples who produced that heritage extended from Native Americans and Spanish colonists, to Mexican settlers and Anglo ranchers, to the more recent "winter Texans" who flock south temporarily each winter to escape the northern states' cold and snow.

The committee chose Edinburg for the museum site when the city made available an old jail built around 1910 of brick and white stucco with a red-tile roof, a windmill out back, and a "hanging tower" with a steel trapdoor inside. In 1967, the museum group incorporated as a nonprofit, tax-exempt organization and it began renovation of the jail in 1968. By the time of the museum's opening, two years later, it had secured collections, planned exhibits, and hired a director to work with a group of talented volunteers.

Wisely, the museum did not set itself up as just a Wild West celebration of supposed desperados who may have dangled in the jail's hanging tower. From the start, the museum established, in writing, a more meaningful and specific purpose, "[T]o maintain exhibits and collections pertaining to the history of the Rio Grande valley, the country and its people, with special emphasis on Hidalgo County. . . . It is the obligation of this museum to assume the responsibilities of the collections which are held in trust for the benefit of the present and future citizens of the county."

Local accountants donated bookkeeping services and other citizens contributed landscaping assistance, display cases, and mannequins, as well as historical artifacts and library materials. Volunteers washed windows, cleaned furniture, and addressed invitations. The museum, open five days a week, drew, in its first year, more than 2,800 visitors. Among the things they saw were temporary exhibits about each of the county's towns.

By 1985, fifteen years later, annual visitation had grown to more than 32,000. A new annex as well as the old jail contained imaginative exhibits on "the Indian Domain," Spanish exploration, border architecture, life on the "Old Ranches," and the way "Old Town" was near the turn of the twentieth century. The exhibits made use of historical photos and maps in juxtaposition with early-day tools, household implements, ranching equipment, mercantile displays, clothing, weapons, and religious artifacts. The museum made itself, in its own words, "a place where you can touch time."

In addition, depending on age and special interests, visitors could do research in the museum's archives of materials on the region's history, hear its regular lecturers, take in its puppet shows and film series, and read the monthly newsletter and books it published on the region. If you were a student in school, a senior citizen in a nursing home, or the program director of a chamber of commerce or civic club, the museum would bring "outreach" programs to you.

At the museum itself, an elevator made exhibits accessible to disabled visitors, and trained guides helped explain the artifacts, which by then totaled more than 15,000 items. New acquisitions were cleaned and stored in accordance with basic rules of conservation, which included keeping artifacts away from fluorescent lights and direct sunlight and maintaining levels of temperature and relative humidity appropriate to prevent deterioration.

A board of eighteen citizens governed the museum, each serving a three-year term, with six trustees changing every year. They hired a staff, which by 1985 included five full-time employees: an executive director, a curator of exhibits, a curator of collections, a building supervisor, and an administrative assistant. The museum also had four part-time staff members and more than sixty active volunteers, who gave more than 7,000 hours of service annually and in-kind services worth $23,800.

The museum developed a Heritage Associates program to increase community involvement and a Museum Guild to help raise money through such special events as an annual "Heritage Round-Up" festival. The county government provided 46 percent of the museum's budget, and the city of Edinburg another 9 percent. The rest came from individual contributions and from earned income of various kinds, including sales in a museum store.

The museum also made use of other kinds of resources. Early on, it took advantage of onsite consultants available from and through the Museum and Field Services Department of the Texas Historical Commission, a state agency headquartered in Austin. Staff members of the museum attended short-term training programs, such as the periodic Winedale Seminars on museum operations. They also participated in meetings of the Texas Association of Museums, and former executive director Fran Alger served on the national council of the American Association of Museums (AAM).

After another ten to fifteen years of operations, the museum took more leaps forward by renovating its facilities, adding a 22,500-square-foot wing, creating new exhibits, and raising its endowment fund to more than $1.2 million. In 2003, it changed its name to the Museum of South Texas History, reflecting its ability to carry out an expanded mission that called for "preserving and presenting the borderland heritage of South Texas and northeastern Mexico." The annual operating budget by then exceeded $900,000, with roughly one-third coming from county and city governments, one-third from earned income, and one-third from special fund-raising. The board, now expanded to twenty-four, received fund-raising and other help from an advisory council of ten; and a staff, which had expanded to thirteen, worked with approximately fifty volunteers. Most staff members had served for several years, providing a degree of stability that Executive Director Shan Rankin called "a huge factor in the museum's progress." The region's growth has greatly benefited the museum, which has kept up by creating a set of programs that involve the evolving community and make the museum meaningful to people of many backgrounds and ages. "We started with nothing. We didn't even have a shoestring," states an early participant in the museum. "The continued growth of our museum is due to the enthusiasm and support of thousands of people in this area."

The Hidalgo story illustrates what is possible. The exceptional success of this familiar kind of museum, committed to the history of a geographical region, gives encouragement to all. But as you plan your museum, someone else's success provides an example for study, not for precise emulation. There are all kinds of "good" museums, small as well as large, carrying out a wide range of missions in ways that creatively vary. No formula will produce a successful museum; that comes from adding creative imagination and persistent determination to an understanding of museum operational basics. This book can serve as a continuing reminder of the latter. If you can provide the rest, all of us who love museums will be grateful.

For More Information

On museum evaluation, the following are useful:

- Baril, Gérald, *Know Your Visitors: Survey Guide*, Société des musées Québécois/Musée de la civilization, 2001

- Committee on Audience Research and Evaluation, *Introduction to Museum Evaluation*, AAM Resource Report/Committee on Audience Research and Evaluation, 1999

- Diamond, Judy, *Practical Evaluation Guide: Tools for Museums and Other Information Educational Settings*, AASLH/AltaMira Press, 1999

- Serrell, Beverly, *Paying Attention: Visitors and Museum Exhibitions*, AAM, 1998

Also, the following technical leaflet from the American Association for State and Local History (AASLH) is pertinent to evaluation:

- *Charting the Impact of Museum Exhibitions and Programs* (2004)

On connecting with museums' communities, the following are helpful:

- AAM, *America's Museums: Building Community*, AAM Communications Kit, 1999

- AAM, *Mastering Civic Engagement: A Challenge to Museums*, AAM, 2002

- AAM, *A Museums and Community Toolkit*, AAM, 2002

- Archibald, Robert R., *A Place to Remember: Using History to Build Community*. AASLH/AltaMira Press, 1999

- Fischer, Daryl K., ed., *Museums, Trustees and Communities: Building Reciprocal Relationships*, AAM/Museum Trustee Association, 1997

- Hamilton-Sperr, Portia, *Museums in the Life of a City: Strategies for Community Partnerships*, AAM, 1995

- Hamilton-Sperr, Portia, *Museums in the Social and Economic Life of the City*, AAM, 1996

On continued planning, the following technical leaflet from AASLH is useful.

- *Process for Effective Idea Development* (189)

The following are some publications to stimulate more thinking about museums, their purposes, and their possibilities:

- Carr, David, *The Promise of Culture Institutions*, AASLH/AltaMira Press, 2003

- Falk, John H., and Lynn D. Dierking, *The Museum Experience*, Whalesback Books, 1992

- George, Gerald, *Visiting History: Arguments over Museums and Historic Sites*, AAM, 1990

- Hudson, Kenneth, *Museums of Influence*, Cambridge University Press, 1987

- *Museums for the New Millennium,* AAM/Smithsonian Institution Center for Museum Studies, 1997

- Rosenzweig, Roy, and David Thelen, *The Presence of the Past: Popular Uses of History in American Life,* Columbia University Press, 1998

- Weil, Stephen E., *A Cabinet of Curiosities: Inquiries into Museums and Their Prospects,* Smithsonian Institution Press, 1995

- Weil, Stephen E., *Making Museums Matter,* Smithsonian Institution Press, 2002

- Weil, Stephen E., *Rethinking the Museum and Other Meditations,* Smithsonian Institution Press, 1990

PART III

SOME BASIC DOCUMENTS

A

Basic Organization Chart

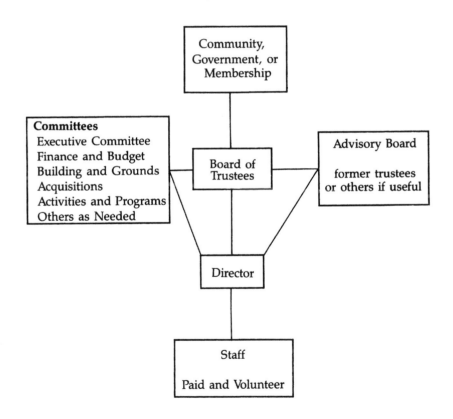

B

Board Membership
Responsibilities Agreement

A volunteer Board of Trustees governs the [name of museum] and is legally responsible for all its actions. This is the "job description" for Board members. Its purpose is to clarify what Board membership involves and to help Board members focus their efforts for the benefit of the organization.

A member of the Board of the [name of museum] will be expected to:

1. Support and endorse the mission statement:

   [insert mission statement]

2. Complete a term of office.

   [explain length of a term, limits on number of terms, and number of terms expiring annually to provide continuity on the Board]

3. Attend Board meetings regularly throughout the year, notifying the president or director in advance if an absence is necessary. A Board member may no longer serve after more than three consecutive unexcused absences.

4. Stay informed about basic policy areas and concerns, and ask probing questions when further information is needed to make reasonable decisions.

5. Share names of potential donors and volunteers with the Board and staff.

6. Contribute to meeting the museum's financial needs in proportion to his or her personal and/or professional resources.

7. Certify that she or he has no conflict or duality of interest or expectation of personal gain from Board service and museum activities.

I agree that the expectations listed above are reasonable for Board members of the [name of museum], and if I become unable or unwilling to carry out these responsibilities, I will resign.

_____

Signature   Date

_____

Name

C

Sample Museum Bylaws

The bylaws presented here are not meant to be copied by every museum. Each museum is different and bylaws must vary to reflect individual museum situations. The following example is merely an illustration for use by a museum in considering how it wishes to organize and what to cover in its bylaws. Assistance with the content and wording of your bylaws from an attorney familiar with applicable laws of your state or other governmental jurisdiction is highly recommended.

Anytown Community Museum Bylaws

Article I

Organization and Location

Section 1.0. The Anytown Community Museum is a _____ nonprofit Corporation with its principal office in the City of _____ in _____County, _____ (state).

Article II

Purpose

Section 2.0. The Corporation's purposes are as set forth in its Articles of Incorporation, which were approved by _____ on _____ (date). The general purpose shall be to collect, preserve, and exhibit objects of value for understanding the history, art, and natural environment of _____ (region).

Article III

Management

Section 3.0. The management of this Corporation shall be vested in a Board of Trustees (hereinafter called the "Board") consisting of not more than _____ members to be elected as prescribed in Section 3.1.

Section 3.1. The terms of one-third (⅓) of the Members of the Board shall expire at each Annual Meeting; their successors shall be elected by the Board at its preceding regular January quarterly meeting, to take office at the next Annual Meeting. A Member's regular term shall be three (3) years, or until a successor is duly qualified. No Member shall be elected to more than two (2) successive full terms. However, an immediate Past President may be elected for an additional successive one-year (1) term on the Board.

Section 3.2. Candidates for Board Membership shall be recommended by a Nominating Committee in consultation with the Executive Committee of the Board and the Director of the Museum, who shall give consideration to the Museum's needs and to representation of various community interests and groups.

Section 3.3. Any Member of the Board who is absent from three (3) meetings in succession without presenting satisfactory explanations shall be deemed to have resigned from the Board and shall cease to be a Member thereof, though eligible for reinstatement by majority vote of the Board. In the event of such a vacancy, or of any other vacancy on the Board, it may elect a successor at any duly convened meeting.

Section 3.4. The Annual Meeting of the Board shall be held on the first Tuesday in April of each year. The Board shall have quarterly meetings on the first Tuesdays of January, April, July, and October. A special meeting shall be called by the Secretary upon written request by seven (7) Members of the Board, and written notice thereof shall be sent to all Members of the Board at least five (5) days prior to the day set for such a meeting. Written notice of the Annual Meeting shall be sent to all Members of the Board at least ten (10) days prior to the day set for such meeting. The Secretary shall serve, or attend to the serving of, all notices.

Section 3.5. The meetings of the Board and all of its Committees shall be conducted according to the latest revision of *Robert's Rules of Order,* but it shall be necessary for a quorum of the Board or any of its Committees to act. A quorum for any such meeting shall be a majority of those entitled to receive notice of the meeting.

Section 3.6. The Board shall assume overall management of the Corporation. It shall receive and act upon all reports of Committees, Officers, and the Director. It shall determine policies of the Museum and take responsibility for its finances and for ethical standards applicable to its activities.

Section 3.7. The Board shall have an Executive Committee, which may act for the Board between meetings thereof. The Executive Committee shall be composed of seven (7) Members, who shall be the officers, the immediate Past President, and one (1) Member-at-large.

Section 3.8. The Board may from time to time appoint ex officio Members as it desires. All ex officio appointments shall terminate at the Annual Meeting of the Board following appointment, and no ex officio Member shall be entitled to vote or be counted as part of a quorum.

Article IV

Officers

Section 4.0. The Officers of the Corporation shall be a President, a First Vice President, a Second Vice President, a Secretary, and a Treasurer, each of whom shall be elected for a term of one (1) year or until a successor is duly qualified.

Section 4.1. No Officer shall be eligible for reelection after serving two (2) terms in office until at least one (1) year shall have expired after her or his last term of office.

Section 4.2. At least sixty (60) days prior to the Board's regular quarterly January meeting, the President shall appoint a Nominating Committee consisting of five (5) Members of the Board. This committee shall investigate the qualifications and availability of persons who might serve as Officers and shall report its recommendations for such positions by letter to the Board at least thirty (30) days prior to its January meeting.

Section 4.3. Additional nominations may be made by any Member of the Board with the consent of the nominee. The Officers shall be elected by majority vote of the Board at its regular January quarterly meeting, and the Officers so elected shall take office at the following Annual Meeting.

Section 4.4. The duties of the Officers shall be the following.

Section 4.41. President: The President shall preside at all meetings of the Board and its Executive Committee. He or she shall appoint all Committees and shall be ex officio a member of each Committee. She or he shall also perform all the usual functions of the President of a _____ non-profit Corporation.

Section 4.42. First Vice President: In the event of the absence of the President or the President's inability or refusal to carry out such duties, the First Vice President shall assume the President's Duties. Also, he or she shall chair one of the standing Committees.

Section 4.43. Second Vice President: In the event of the absence of the First Vice President or her or his inability or refusal to carry out such duties, the Second Vice President shall assume such duties. Also, he or she shall chair one of the standing Committees.

Secretary 4.44: Secretary: The Secretary shall provide notices of meetings and, with assistance from the Director, shall take minutes of meetings of the Board, which shall be submitted at each subsequent meeting for Board approval and

kept on file at a place designated by the Executive Committee. The Secretary, with assistance from the President and
the Director, shall be responsible for formal communications from and to the Corporation.

Section 4.45: Treasurer: The Treasurer, with assistance from the
Director, shall keep an accurate record of all monies received and disbursed by the Corporation, financial records
to be kept on file at a place designated by the Executive
Committee. The Treasurer shall deposit all monies received
in one or more banks and/or savings and loan institutions
located in the city of _____, to the credit of the
Corporation, and she or he shall make investments in such
assets as are approved by the Board. All such investments
shall be in the name of the Corporation. Upon the approval
of the Board or its Executive Committee, the Treasurer shall
use the available funds of the Corporation to pay all of its
just bills. At each Annual Meeting, the Treasurer shall submit a written report for the fiscal year just ended.

Section 4.46. Vacancies: A vacancy in any office, whatever the
cause, shall be filled for the remainder of the current term
by the Board at a duly convened meeting if the notice
thereof contains advisement of such election.

Article V

Museum Director

Section 5.0. The Board may appoint a Director, who shall be in
charge of the operation of the Museum. The Director shall be
responsible for its administration and its activities in accordance with policies established by the Board. He or she shall
have authority to employ and dismiss members of the Staff in
accordance with policies and budgets approved by the Board.
At the Annual Meeting, the Director shall submit an Annual
Report on the condition and activities of the Museum, and she
or he shall make recommendations regarding the condition
and activities. The Director shall submit informal progress
reports at the meetings of the Board and of its Executive

Committee, and he or she shall call to their attention any matters requiring action or notice.

Article VI

Committees

Section 6.0. The Board may by resolution designate one (1) or more Committees. Each Committee may exercise powers as provided by the Board. Each Committee shall have such name as the Board may determine.

Section 6.1. The Committees shall keep regular minutes of their proceedings and report to the Board when required.

Section 6.2. The Board's Standing Committees may include Acquisitions, Activities and Programs, Building and Grounds, Exhibits, Finance and Budget, Membership, Memorials, Personnel, Public Relations, Standing Rules, and others as needed.

Section 6.3. The chairs of the Standing Committees shall be members of the Board. Standing Committees shall consist of at least two (2) members of the Board and others deemed qualified by the President.

Section 6.4. The membership of all other Committees, which may include Board Members, shall be in such number and for such terms as the President shall designate.

Article VII

Advisory Board

Section 7.0. Members of an Advisory Board may be nominated by the Executive Committee and elected by the Board at its Annual Meeting. Persons appointed to the Advisory Board shall have the ability to make specific, needed contributions to the Museum and its activities. Reelection to the Advisory Board shall be only after service on one of its Committees or after contributions in support of the Museum and its activities. Members of the Advisory Board shall not be entitled to vote on the policies and management of the Corporation or be counted for quorum purposes.

Section 7.1. Members of the Advisory Board shall attend the Annual Meeting of the Corporation. A regular meeting of the Advisory Board shall be held on the second Tuesday in October of each year.

Article VIII

Financial Matters

Section 8.0. No funds of the Corporation shall be invested or expended without authorization of the Board.

Section 8.1. The Board shall designate the Corporation's fiscal year. The books of account of the Corporation shall be balanced and audited by a Certified Public Accountant at the close of each fiscal year or other regularly designated period, as permitted by law.

Section 8.2. The Director, and other employees as determined by the Board, shall from time to time be bonded in amounts, for purposes, and with corporate sureties acceptable to the Board.

Article IX

Amendments

Section 9.0. Alterations, amendments, or repeals of these bylaws may be made by a majority of the Members of the Board entitled to vote at any Annual or Quarterly Meeting, if the notice thereof contains a statement of the proposed alteration, amendment, or repeal.

Article X

Annual Reports

Section 10.0. Each Officer and Committee chairperson shall render annual, written reports of the activities of their respective Offices or Committees. Such reports shall be filed with the Secretary at the Annual Meeting. An Annual Report of the Museum shall be published as soon as possible after the Annual Meeting.

Article XI

Dissolution

Section 11.0. Should the museum at any time permanently cease to function, the buildings and real property shall remain in place and be turned over to the _____ County Court to be used at its discretion for other educational purposes.

Section 11.1. Artifacts and personalty that are the permanent property of the Museum shall be transferred to another museum or educational institution. Should there be outstanding debts owed by the Museum, sufficient of said personalty may be sold to satisfy creditors.

Section 11.2. Personal artifacts on loan to the museum must be returned to the donors as authorized by the signatures of the _____ County Judge and the President of the Board of Trustees.

Section 11.3. After the Corporation permanently abandons the operation of the Museum, the endowment fund as created and described shall revert in full to _____ County to be used by any one or more educational institutions, such institutions to be named by the County Commissioners Court, subject to applicable state laws.

D

Typical Museum Budget List

Each museum is unique, so budget line items will vary according to the type of museum and the activities it undertakes. Therefore, the following basic budget should not be considered all-inclusive. It can suggest things you might otherwise overlook, but make your own list by considering all sources of potential income for your particular museum and all expenses for the particular activities you plan.

INCOME
Government and/or Private Contributions
Membership Dues
Admission Charges
Museum Store Sales
Special Events
Program Income
Income from Investments

EXPENSES
Salaries
Payroll Taxes
Fringe Benefits
Conservation
Utilities
Maintenance

Office Supplies
Supplies for Educational and Other Programs
Exhibit Expense
Insurance
Museum Store Expense
Publications (including brochures and other public relations
    materials)
Vehicles (including maintenance and fuel)
Cleaning Supplies
Legal, Accounting, and Consultant Fees
Professional Memberships and Subscriptions
Staff Travel

Remember to provide in your budget up-front expenses for any special event, museum store stock, and programs or publications from which you expect income later.

E

Sample Position Description for a Director

Job Title:	Director.
Classification:	[if within a unit of government].
Education:	Bachelor's degree minimum and advanced degree preferred in museum studies or a discipline related to the museum's mission and collections.
Experience, Skills and Knowledge:	Organizational and administrative ability. Ability to initiate programs, train and motivate people, coordinate activities, speak publicly, and deal effectively with community groups and interests. Knowledge of and interest in the subject matter dealt with by the museum. Understanding of museum development and ability to communicate that understanding to the Board and to stakeholders, supporters, and others outside the museum. Minimum of five years' experience in museum work. Previous managerial or supervisory experience preferred.
Position and Description:	1. Responsible for recruiting, orienting, training, motivating, and evaluating staff members including volunteers. 2. Responsible for developing plans and budgets for consideration by the Board,

and for their implementation when approved.

3. Responsible for establishing and maintaining appropriate records, forms, procedures, and practices relating to collections, personnel, purchasing, and general administration.

4. Responsible for facilities security, visitor safety, and maintenance of facilities and equipment.

5. Responsible for developing and carrying out all ongoing activities and special programs of the museum within budgets and policies approved by the Board.

6. Will attend all meetings of the Board and its committees, maintain liaison with them, provide financial and other reports as requested, and maintain public relations broadly in the community.

7. Will assist the Board in fund-raising activities and in presentations to sources of support.

Compensation: Salary, medical insurance, retirement-plan contributions, sick leave, vacation time, and expense-paid opportunities for professional development such as participation in annual meetings of relevant professional associations.

F

Sample Certificate of Gift

CERTIFICATE OF GIFT

Name of Donor _____

Address _____

_____

Description of Gift:

I (we), being the sole legal owner(s) of the property described above, hereby give to the Anytown Community Museum, for its use and benefit without restriction as to use or disposition, the property described above. In addition, I (we) give all copyright and associated rights I (we) have. To the best of my (our) knowledge, I (we) have good and complete right, title, and interest including all transferred copyright, trademark, and related interests to give. I (we) have no objections to my (our) name(s) appearing as donor(s) in connection with this gift in Museum records, publications, and other descriptions.

Signature _____
Signature _____
Date _____

G

Standard Object
Cataloging Record

ANYTOWN COMMUNITY MUSEUM

_____ Gift
_____ Purchase $ _____
_____ Exchange
_____ Field Collection
_____ Loan

Catalog [or Accession] No. _____ Received by _____
Date of accession _____
Object name _____
Materials _____
Maker/artist/manufacturer _____
Place of Origin _____
Description _____

_____

_____

_____

Condition _____

_____

Value _____

Dimensions _____

Name, address, telephone number, and e-mail address of immediate source _____

_____

_____

_____

Dates of ownership _____

Previous owner_____ Dates _____

Previous owner_____ Dates _____

Documents accompanying acquisition _____

_____

Donor information (donation's use, age, association with places, individuals, or events) _____

_____

_____

_____

Location _____ Date _____

Accepted by _____* Accessioned by _____

Cataloged by _____

Bibliographic, photographic, and documentary cross-references

_____

_____

_____

Restrictions _____

Remarks _____

_____

_____

*Include reference to page of minutes of Board action

Index

accreditation, 9, 10; accredited
museums and, xiv
African American Museum
(Philadelphia), xii
Alexander & Baldwin Sugar
Museum, xi, 66
Alger, Fran, 123
Alutiiq Museum and
Archaeological Repository
(Kodiak, Alaska), xii
American Association of
Museums (AAM), xiv, 9, 10,
15, 16, 18, 19, 45, 105, 123;
accreditation program and, 16;
affiliated museum
organizations and, 17; *Aviso*
and, 16; Historic House
Museums Professional Interest
Council and, 17; marketing
and public relations, 42, 43;
Museum Assessment Program
(MAP) and, 16; Museum
Management Committee and,
17; *Museum News* and, 16;
publications of, 10, 16;
resource reports of, 11, 42, 43;

Small Museum
Administrators' Committee
and, 17; Small Museums
Committee and, 16; traveling
exhibits and, 68; Trustees
Committee and, 15
American Association for State
and Local History (ASSLH), xi,
xii, 14, 16, 18, 19, 45, 105;
Board Organizer/Orientation
Kit and, 16–17; collections
management and, 101;
conservation and, 96; *Dispatch*
and, 16; earned revenue and,
42; exhibits and, 100; Field
Services Alliance and, 14, 17;
heritage projects and, 53–54;
historic house care and, 97;
Historic House Museum
Issues and Operations and, 16;
Historic House Task Force
and, 16; *History News* and, 16;
history of, 16; local records
and, 54; marketing and public
relations and, 43; mentoring
program of, 16; museum

of, 8–9; development of, 45, 46,
47, 64, 107, 115; donors and,
38; e-mail discussion groups
and, 17, 18; endowment funds
and, 35; ethics and, 109, 110;
evaluation of, 64, 117, 118, 124;
exhibit catalogs and, 37;
festivals and, 47; field-service
programs and, 14; financial
planning and, 33, 40, 41;
financial reports and, 116, 119;
focus groups and, 38; fund-
raising and, 7, 35, 36, 38, 39;
heritage projects and, 52, 53;
human resources and, 103; in-
kind contributions and, 37;
insurance and, 71;
interpretation and, 5, 8, 49, 92,
93, 98; marketing and, 39, 40,
42; mission of, 40, 63, 64, 65,
66, 67, 72, 120; museum
consultant program and, 14;
museum stores and, 37, 42;
national organizations and,
19–26; number of, xi; objects,
caring for, 6; objects, respect
for, 7; operations and, 63, 75;
organization and operation,
principle of, 3; organization
chart and, *129*; overhead
expenses and, 34; physical
facilities and, 7, 63, 69, 72, 73;
planning committee report
and, 118; planning of, 13,
63–64, 118, 119; political
connections, maintaining of,
117; preservations and, 58, 59;
public, reaching out to, 64, 116,
117; publications of, 37;
publicity committee and, 119;
public trust laws and, 33;

records, maintaining of, 6;
regional museum
organizations, 26–28;
registration and, 5; renting of,
37; research and, 4, 5, 8, 64;
respect, as principle, 8, 10;
responsibilities and, 10, 63;
revenue sources and, 39;
secretary of the board reports
and, 116, 119; security and, 6,
63, 71, 72, 73; seminars and,
18; special projects and, 34;
staff and, 7, 79; stakeholders
and, 117; strategic planning
and, 7; support, assessing of,
38; support, sources of, 15, 16,
17; surveys, use of, 38;
targeted audiences of, 34; tax-
exempt status and, 37; tourism
and, 34; universities and, 18;
volunteers and, 38, 79, 80, 108,
111–12; websites and, 93;
workshops and, 18
museum stores, 37, 42
Museum Stores Association, 37
museum studies, 18, 19

National Afro-American
    Museum and Cultural Center
    (Dayton, Ohio), 65
National Aquarium (Baltimore), xi
National Conference of State
    Museum Associations, 17
National Council on Public
    History, 18
National Information Center for
    Local Government Records, 54
National Institute for the
    Conservation of Cultural
    Property, 54
National Park Service, xii, 18, 48

About the Authors

Gerald George was director of the American Association for State and Local History, director of the National Historical Publications and Records Commission, and director of communications for the National Archives and Records Administration. He served on the board of the American Association of Museums, the editorial board of the *Encyclopedia of the American West*, and the Leadership Team of the National Archives. He is the author of numerous articles and of the book *Visiting History: Arguments over Museums and Historic Sites* (1990), and was managing editor of *The States and the Nation*, a series of state history books.

Cindy Sherrell-Leo is currently a board member of the Galveston Historical Foundation and chair of the Dickens on the Strand festival. Cindy is special projects director to Southwest Museum Services, Houston and Lone Star Flight Museum, Galveston. For nineteen years Cindy directed the Museum Services Department of the Texas Historical Commission, providing hundreds of consultations to historical commissions and museums. Earlier, Cindy was acting director and business manager of the Laguna Gloria Art Museum, and registrar of the University of Texas Art Museum. Cindy has served on the councils of the American Association of Museums and the American

Association for State and Local History, has been a consultant to the Smithsonian Institution's Office of Museum Programs, has administered the Winedale Museum Seminars, and has frequently spoken to museum conferences.